Where There's Love

"The return of the angels to human consciousness could be one of the greatest surprises of the twentieth century..."

H C Moolenburgh, M D
A Handbook of Angels (C. W. Daniel)

WHERE THERE'S LOVE

the Story of a Community and its Guiding Impulse

Annie Wilson

Gateway Books, Bath

and Interbook Inc, San Leandro, Calif.

First published in 1986
by GATEWAY BOOKS
19 Circus Place,
Bath, BA1 2PW

in the U.S.A.: INTERBOOK Inc,
14895 E. 14th Street,
San Leandro, CA 94577

Set in Palacio 10½ on 12pt by
Mathematical Composition Setters Ltd
of Salisbury, Wilts
Printed and bound in Great Britain
by WBC of Bristol

British Library Cataloguing in Publication Data

Wilson, Annie
    Where there's love: the story of a
    community and its guiding impulse.
    1. Atlanteans
    I. Title
    133   BP605.A/

ISBN 0-946551-27-8

Contents

Acknowledgements

When Tony Neate first invited me to speak, through him, to his guide Helio-Arcanophus, I confess I was apprehensive. It was something out of my experience. After that first meeting I seemed to bathe for a long time in an energy that was full of care and concern—avuncular even— imbued with awe-inspiring humility and with an unmistakable humour. I was deeply moved and I knew I would recognise that energy again. H-A's first words, without prompting, had been to clarify a concept in his teachings about which I had felt uneasy. It was uncanny how much he knew of what I was thinking.

Also at the first meeting H-A assured me that he would always be with me during the writing of this book. If I got stuck, he said, I had only to ask; if I was willing and confident enough to do so. Each time I sat down to work with the teachings I was aware that the energy around me lifted and lightened. H-A confirmed later that 'they' had indeed been helping me, adding that he hoped I didn't mind that help—which again showed extraordinary insight into my character!

I cannot explain exactly how this help manifests, but with such guidance there is somehow an economy of effort, a flow in the structuring and collating that is not present in, say, ordinary journalism. Obviously it is still not easy! From a very deep place in my being I thank H-A for the opportunity and privilege of experiencing this whole new field of awareness.

My thanks, too, of course, to the families of Runnings Park, for their friendship, generosity and hospitality, and not least for sharing the unique *ambience* of Runnings Park itself. I would also like to express my gratitude to Michael Dean whose initial re-editing and compilation of H-A's material saved me a great deal of time and effort! Finally, my special love and thanks to Austin who makes so many things possible.

La Rippe
Switzerland
September 1985

Prelude

Birth Pangs of a New Age

People return to Runnings Park Hotel and Conference Centre time and again. On the surface that is not surprising. The centre, part of what was once a Victorian farm complex built in 1890 as a replica of one of Queen Victoria's farms, is set in seventeen acres, surrounded by trees, and sits seven hundred feet up the slopes of the Worcester Beacon hillside in West Malvern. Its grounds slope westward towards the valley, encompassing three pond-lakes, and on a clear day the view extends thirty-four miles to the Black Mountains in Wales. Sheep graze lazily in the meadows, horses frolic for fun, friendly dogs dash to your feet demanding attention and a family of geese march in touching solidarity towards the middle lake.

The externals are idyllic. But what the guests probably do not realise, not consciously at least, is that they return for another, less obvious reason. What cannot be seen, only intuited, is the special ambience or atmosphere, the energy of Runnings Park, that is expressed through the four couples who own and run it. When Tony and Ann Neate, Henley and Patricia Thomas, David and Diane Furlong and Judy and Mick Jewell moved into Runnings Park four years ago, it was the outcome of a decision made many years earlier. In 1981 they were able finally to fulfil a vision: to live, while in separate family units, within a community.

In one way it was quite a normal decision to make. Today it is relatively common for people to come together to live a lifestyle that suits a new ideal, for mutual growth and to live and work for a higher purpose than just themselves. Community living is not new. What is more unusual is that of this group of eight, six are the core members of a society called *The Atlanteans*. This society was inspired by the spiritual teaching of a discarnate spirit, an initiate guide, known as Helio-Arcanophus—or the initials H-A for short, who began to 'channel' a philosophy of a very fine nature, firstly through Tony Neate thirty years ago, and subsequently through others.

Runnings Park is an act of pure faith. It represents a commitment made to and asked of them by H-A to provide a 'spiritual home' for the Atlanteans, a rooted base within which six people who have chosen to accept the task, can take responsibility for the dissemination of—and more than that, to live—the teachings. This commitment inspires the resonance behind Runnings Park—of which the hotel is a small though materially vital part. And it is this resonance that feeds the atmosphere, that draws more and more to take part in any of the activities that take place there: the healing weekends, the meditation group, seminars on spiritual matters, courses on psychology, stress, astrology, ley energies, art and vegetarian cookery and even the swimming in the indoor pool.

H-A tells us that life on our planet is at a critical stage. Our material evolution has been accelerating in leaps and bounds at a pace which we can no longer control. In itself there is nothing bad in scientific and technical advance: all progressive experience is good, provided it proceeds with balance. Lack of balance is the cause of many of the problems of this planet and much of the illness prevalent today is brought about by a lack of balance in everyday living.

Over the past years man's disregard and disrespect for this planet has increased. He has raped the land, poisoned the seas and polluted the air, seriously affecting the whole balance of nature. The planet is a macrocosm of ourselves and in fairness to man, he has meted out the same treatment to his own body! He does not feed or look after it properly and forces it into all kinds of extreme situations for which it was never designed.

According to H-A any planet is about thought or vibrations on all levels of comprehension, from spirit right down to the physical, and about the harmonizing of those levels of thought. All spirit is created with equal love and consideration by the ultimate thought, the Godhead. Each thought created by the Godhead is able to experience complete freedom and ultimate choice, a choice that allows that spirit to go forward, to meander or go backwards, sideways, up or down. The process of evolution of the spirit is first of all to understand itself and then to learn to understand and respect other thoughts on a similar level and other thoughts on different levels, all experiencing and evolving in different ways.

On this planet there are many forms of spirit experience, not only man in his physical body, says H-A. There is the type of experience gained within a flower or a tree or within the minerals and elements of which the planet is composed. All these different forms need to exist in harmony for the planet as a whole to function in balance. In his attempt to control nature man is surprised when nature reacts unco-operatively. Nature is very tolerant and has allowed man to get away with a great deal, but there are various warning signs. These are evident in the types of disease that prevail at the present time. You cannot ill-treat your physical body indefinitely without some form of mutation occurring.

There is always action, reaction and interaction in all human experience. For example, spending a weekend with friends not only affects the lives of those friends, but the animals who are there to meet you. You eat the food prepared for you. This affects not only the people who have produced it, but creates a greater demand for food in that locality, and uses more light energy and gas. Certain materials wear out a little more quickly so perhaps a forest will have to be dug out of the ground in Africa. One of H-A's prime purposes, he says, has been to try and re-educate man into finding a balanced and respectful relationship with all other forms of existence in God's universe.

We are part of planet Earth and our planet is part of a solar system, which in turn is part of a galaxy. Every thought goes out into the universe for eternity and every thought, action and deed affects the balance of the whole universe. So the kind of abuse we render to this planet has a bearing elsewhere in the solar system and beyond. Often in the past people have questioned the amount of influence man has on the fate of his planet. In fact he has a responsibility which is desperately important. The thoughts and actions of each of us *do* matter: we each exert an influence that has an effect on the whole, for good or ill.

Today there is an ever-increasing influence of things which are in H-A's words 'unbeautiful'. He uses that word carefully, because civilisations which were in other ways advanced have become unhinged by this rather subtle infiltration of the 'unbeautiful'. The medium through which it first begins is 'art' in its broadest sense, and that includes music and literature, plays and any form of creative work. Art is a short cut to the emotions and instead of helping people to understand things which have gentleness and tolerance, the emphasis more and more is placed on violence, horror, shock and sensationalism, which jangles and disrupts and causes disharmony.

Thinking becomes programmed to the need for brutal and destructive entertainment, and the pace quickens until there is no time to think of things which are simple and beautiful. Love becomes almost a dirty word. In seeking lazier forms of entertainment people are channelled into a zombie-ism, forfeiting their individuality.

Governments find their people easier to control when the man in the street does as he is told, so their best policy is to discourage him from thinking and feed him with just sufficient information to make him useful in an industrial or economic capacity, but no more.

The man in the street today, therefore, is encouraged to watch television every night, through which medium only the 'right' information can be fed. He is encouraged to lead a happy and contented life in which he does not interfere in any way with the will of the ruling powers who are plunging the world headlong into catastrophe. And why is all this happening? Because, like the people whom they lead and whom they do not encourage to think, those leaders are not thinking of the future. They are thinking of the power they can hold over their fellow men *now*.

Such are the problems we are up against, says H-A. All types of negative thinking and behaviour that fan the element of fear are being sponsored and inflamed. The question is, do we have the will and desire to rise above this negativity? Are we apathetic or do we make some effort to bring kindness, fairness and tolerance and balance into our everyday lives? How many of us who read this can honestly admit every mistake we make? asks H-A. How many of us really keep an open mind and do not blind ourselves to the things that we do not want to see?

The planet Earth is reaching a peak in a cycle of evolution. These peaks occur approximately every two thousand years as the earth transits from one solar age to the next. It is now leaving the Piscean age and moving into the Aquarian age, and Earth is about to come under a different form of influence. It will experience a different pattern of behaviour, a different speed of spiritual metabolism. These transitional periods are moments when the energy on the planet is greatly increased and the forces of Light endeavour to present to the planet as a whole the opportunity to restore balance, the balance it is capable of achieving at that particular moment of self-realisation. The whole atmosphere of the planet begins to increase and intensify, providing the possibility for the quickening of experience and a stride forward in evolution.

The changes are transpiring within all of us as well as outside ourselves in the higher spiritual realms, says H-A. Therefore each of us in our own way must reassess who and what we are, making certain that we are giving love and light to ourselves so that we are healing ourselves within. We need to make contact with that spiritual aspect of our being, our inner source, that will bring enlightenment to help us become more harmonious in every aspect of ourselves. As we heal ourselves so we will heal the planet, and as we heal the planet so we will heal ourselves. It is in our hands. It is our responsibility. The future of the planet is not rigidly preordained: it follows a certain pattern, but mankind has the power—and the choice—to shape it either way.

H-A has made it clear that for any new impulse of harmony there must be change and transmutation of all that is negative and discordant on every level. This will be traumatic for many people, for if a person is fixed in his thinking and not flowing in harmony with cosmic law, the new impulse of Light will provoke a crisis which will have far-reaching effects on him on every level, from the physical to the spiritual. This will happen not only to individuals, but to countries, to continents and to the whole planet.

H-A appeared to Tony Neate thirty years ago so that an understanding could be released on the planet, an understanding related to this particular time that would merge with other beliefs and understandings, to help a group of people who had incarnated for this purpose, and to enable this planet to more easily transit from one age to the next. His aim has been to bring through a philosophy and love and light and hope; a philosophy that is relevant to this transition period into the Aquarian age.

It is a contemporary teaching that inspires the breaking down of attitudes that have become too fixed, encouraging men and women to become free thinkers and responsible for their own destinies.

It is a truly wonderful universe, says H-A, and although man is sometimes depressed in his efforts to harmonise on this planet, those who are trying to guide him feel that so much more would be achieved if only man could recognise his achievements for what they are without wanting to boost them through feelings of insecurity. He would find his experiences here so much more fulfilling. Part of his evolution at the present time is to find that fulfillment, to begin to move beyond the need for security and its resultant feeling of insecurity, for both are illusions.

There are many forces of Light being brought to bear on this planet at this moment, of which mine is only one. We all try to provide an aspect of truth that is going to help someone. It is like looking at Nelson's Column. Imagine you are in an air balloon at the bottom of the Column. Rise up ten feet and you see a few paving stones. It is a wonderful experience because you are looking at absolute truth. Go up a little higher and you see all of Trafalgar Square: the people, pigeons, buses and cars. It is quite remarkable because at that moment you are experiencing absolute truth. Move up even further and you see the whole of Greater London: its people living, working and dying.

That is absolute truth. Evolution is seeing the same truth but from an ever wider and more objective perspective. There is a place for all levels of understanding, all have a role to play. We all interact with each other and must live in acceptance of other people's ideas. Who is to say what is right?

As I said when I first spoke through a sensitive, if I can help one spirit to find itself then I am truly happy. It does not matter how many teachings there are. It does not matter that they are all different. If each one of us sees the universe from our own stage of evolution, we see the whole in our particular way, so it would not matter if there were 5,000 million philosophies or religious sects on this planet, provided each one loved and respected the others and acknowledged that the others had their place just as much as it did. Only the Godhead itself has absolute truth and absolute understanding of truth, and no one can see that, feel it or become at one with it until he has actually reached that level of understanding himself.

The true wisdom of Almighty God is something that truly transcends mortal words, mortal understanding. It is beyond colour, sound, density, feeling or symbol. It is something so fine, so delicate and yet all-embracing. It is within each of us; for we are part of the whole, created by the whole, experiencing and adding to the whole.

This book, then, is a living exposition of how one group of spirits has come together to enter into a group experience, who have taken responsibility in their particular way to help in the healing of the planet—and above all, of the philosophy that inspired them.

Note: Please note that quotations from H-A are set in a smaller typeface in a narrower column than Annie Wilson's text.

PART ONE

Getting Off the Ground

Chapter One

The Reluctant Medium

Religious education at Tony Neate's school in Croydon during the war was a simple matter. For those who were Church of England the local vicar came round to teach once a week; for those who were Roman Catholic there was a priest. Everyone else, including Tony Neate, was classified OD—other denominations—and went to play football. It was a privilege jealously guarded!

At home things were different. Tony's father was a "fanatical primitive Methodist". Each Sunday the family, at father's instigation, was subjected to all the church services on the radio. When the clergymen said 'let us pray', everything stopped. Tony remembers one particular Sunday, when his mother dropped a spoon on the kitchen floor and his father went into a raging temper. If this is God, he thought, thank God I don't believe in Him!

A querulous beginning for matters spiritual. Father's enthusiasm for religion had produced an agnostic son. As for spiritualism and psychism, which was relegated by father to the end of the pier, here the scepticism rubbed off. In 1950, aged twenty, Tony married Jacqueline Murry Hope, whom he had met in the Royal Air Force during National Service. When Jackie and two friends, Edwin Naylor and Mary Prestage, began to play around with the 'glass on the table' game (equivalent of the modern ouija board) in their flat in Streatham Hill, Tony was determined to prove it did not work. He was reluctant to become involved with this "stuff and nonsense". One evening, however, they did persuade him to put his finger on the glass and it seemed to work better. Quite dramatic things happened.

"I remember one night a question was asked by someone who came in to see us," says Tony. "It was quite obvious that whoever we had contacted through the glass did not like him. We saw the glass fly off the table and hit the man in the chest with so much force that he went straight over the back of his chair in fright. There was no way any one of us could have done that. I think now this is an extremely dangerous practice and we advise people not to do it: you can pick up mischievous spirits close to the earth. We spend a lot of time now trying to help people who have got themselves in trouble doing that sort of thing."

And yet, he admits, if he had not put his finger on the glass, a whole world might not have opened. The group egged him on to try other forms of psychism, like psychometry, which one of the group had heard about. In psychometry a psychic becomes sensitised to the vibrations of an object and can read its history. When he first tried to do so nothing happened. Then Jackie suggested he focus on a key or symbol. He visualised the screen of a television set in his mind's eye, turned on the set and repeated what he saw. The pictures appeared to be correct.

What came through provided information, help and interest to the people concerned. On reflection, says Tony, it was like a primitive form of counselling. People had problems in their lives or at work and through the object he could give warnings of what might happen if things did not change. The weakness of the exercise was in picking up the vibrations of someone who had previously owned the object. Once, when Tony was given a pair of earrings and asked to do a reading, the owner said the reading was totally wrong. Instinctively he knew the answer. He felt the reading was for a stronger personality than the present owner and when he suggested this he was told they had been given to her by her mother, to whom the reading fitted perfectly.

He practised a great deal of psychometry. At least, he felt, he was not doing any harm and he did not charge people for the service, since he considered it would be morally wrong to take money for what appeared to be a free gift. He also made the exercise as hard as possible for himself, asking for objects that could not be defined by sex. If he was given earrings, for example, he knew his subject was a girl (in those days!).

People began to hear of Tony on the grapevine. He was gaining a reputation for his psychic work and had to accept that he did have some sort of psychic gift. Even so, Jackie and the others had much more confidence in his ability as a psychic than Tony did himself. At Jackie's suggestion he went—highly sceptical—to see a medium, Marjorie Wheble, who in turn sent him to a Mrs Stobart, in Sanderstead, Surrey. Mrs Stobart served him tea and scones in the drawing room, decorated entirely in funereal purple, and insisted on showing him photographs of her actress daughter, who had died in mysterious circumstances by falling down a lift-shaft at an all-night party given by Tyrone Power. By the conclusion of a most bizarre afternoon, when the intimidating Mrs Stobart felt inspired to do a trance for him, Tony felt quite alarmed. Yet the trance proved to be one of the most profound experiences of his life.

The spirit guide who spoke through Mrs Stobart announced that Tony had a mission for which he would need to be prepared. He was going to work in the psychic field; he would be a medium and bring through a significant teaching. Other prophetic things the spirit told him subsequently proved accurate. "At the time it meant very little to me," says Tony. "But I did get goose pimples! I realised many things had to be awoken."

It was several years before Tony experienced his first

trance. One evening the friends were giving him a psychometry 'test'. Jackie remembers they presented him with an envelope. Inside were a few pieces of floorboard from the Stoll theatre next door. Tony tuned in and saw a gentleman riding in a coach in the 1890s alongside a row of houses. The houses suddenly fell down and in their place he saw a theatre being built. Later they checked the story and the gentleman was obviously Sir Oswald Stoll, founder of the Stoll theatre. They were able to confirm that there had been houses on the original site.

A moment later Tony, who thought he had fallen asleep, saw the others looking at him in great surprise. "Something that claimed to be a spirit had spoken through me. I had done my first trance." This first guide was René Teillard, a French lawyer. He said he had come to help them by giving them material evidence, as he was nearer to the earth than the more philosophic guides who would talk to them later. On another occasion René even helped them with a law case. A friend of the group had a legal problem, which she considered to be unjustified. René gave advice that seemed to go against the facts of the situation, but the friend followed it and avoided serious trouble.

Over the next year or two Tony tuned into all kinds of guides. They often produced highly evidential information, which was helpful to many people. The second guide who came through was the German psychiatrist Sigmund Freud. He told them about a certain book written in German from which he quoted something, giving chapter and page. After much research Edwin finally found the book in the archives of a London library and the quotation was found as given. Another spirit, Australian singer Dame Nellie Melba, told them about a performance she had once given in Brussels. This was checked and found to be true. She also helped Jackie, who had trained as a singer at the Royal College of Music, with some technical singing points.

To throw a little light on this transition you now call 'death', but which should be retitled 'rebirth' or 'reawakening'; there *is* no death, only transformation. Does a tree die in winter? Everything about its appearance suggests that it does, but we know that it has simply withdrawn into itself and is quietly preparing to re-emerge in the coming years. The entire process is no more than a breathing in and a breathing out again. This occurs in all things, from the smallest particle to the universe itself.

As man has become more deeply embedded in matter, he has gradually lost sight of who he is, where he comes from, why he visits Earth and where he goes to when each phase of the adventure is over. What an appalling waste it would be if death really were the end of a human being! To think of all that effort and experience and creativity being thrown away. But nature abhors waste as much as it abhors a vacuum, so nothing is discarded, everything is recycled. When you discard your physical body, as you would a shabby overcoat, the inner, essential you goes back home to the inner planes with all its recent knowledge and experience and skills, its loves and friendships intact.

Most people are quite unaware of the help they receive from the spirit world in the form of inspiration, ideas, protection, guidance and the many so-called coincidences that have a powerful effect on their lives. There are many ways in which discarnate beings are able to help those who are incarnate, to their mutual benefit. Certain spirits act as guides, helping a particular person through his or her Earth life. They are sometimes referred to as 'door-keepers' or guardian angels or controls, and their service is not unrewarded: they too learn from the experience in many instances. In the case of a medium or 'sensitive' they also stand guard when psychic work is being carried out and protect their charges from less evolved spirits that might try to interfere.

It is possible for a guardian angel or guide to change during a lifetime, but this usually only happens when the course of a person's life has been radically altered so that he or she can undertake specific work. Then there are those spirits who may wish to assist someone for a specific purpose, so they attach themselves to that person for a particular period. For example, a guide might give specialised help to someone studying for an examination or researching a project, or to a writer, designer, musician, scientist, engineer, teacher or politician at some key moment. Once sufficient help has been given the spirit will withdraw and turn to others in a similar situation. At one time or another most human beings are helped, not only by their guardian angel or guide but by loved ones, specialists and other spirits with whom they may have established a vital connection on some previous occasion.

By this time Jackie was also emerging as an accomplished psychic in her own right. She was a gifted clairvoyant and practised automatic writing. She and Tony were soon able to cross-check each other's work, yet still Tony was not totally convinced. "One side of me always has been and always will be highly sceptical of psychic matters," he says. "The more you go into it the more you realise how much room there is for error. No medium is infallible. When you give a reading, whatever it is, it is still using the mind and personality of the medium. This has to come through, however conscientious you are."

In addition to these 'professional' misgivings, Tony was extremely apprehensive that the psychic work would be prejudicial to his job at Shell, the multinational oil company where he worked in the accounts department. He was convinced that if they found out he was 'mixed up with a lot of spooks', his livelihood would be in jeopardy. On the other hand, he was happy to go along with the experiences that were confronting him because nothing bad happened that could do any harm. It was worth going on to see what transpired. Besides which it was also exciting.

Describing a trance is like describing how to ride a bike, says Tony. You can't. The psychic faculty is simply a sixth sense, that part of ourselves which can become aware of other dimensions. The purpose of meditation, for example, is to try to find the 'higher self' or inner source, by linking through various levels of consciousness within, each one finer and more subtle. At any one of these levels, a sensitive can link in to the cosmos; can pick up other forms of experience and receive guidance.

A trance is a certain state of relaxation in which you become conscious of spirit guides around. The level of vibration on which this occurs depends on the harmony, purity and intentions of the sensitive and of the group of people who have come together to focus their thought. At a fairly low level there might be 'Aunt Flo' on the other side who can find a lost handkerchief. On a finer wavelength there is the possibility of tuning into more positive information. This is why Tony prefers to be called a sensitive rather than a medium which he feels gives the wrong connotation to the way he is working. A medium conjures up the image of a 'Madame Arcate' type of communication.* The finer a spirit, the higher the 'spirit plane' from which it comes.

When a spirit first leaves the body it is often 'lost' for a while. It is no longer hampered by a physical body, one that perhaps caused it much suffering. It is like being suddenly released from prison after many years 'inside'. The spirit may be met by friends who will explain what has happened or, if it is undeveloped, it

---

* Madam Arcate was the character played by Margaret Rutherford in the first performances of Noel Coward's play *Blithe Spirit*.

may not realise that it has passed over and will continue in a state of mind to live as it did while incarnate. It may roam around its old home for some days after death, distressed that its loved ones ignore it, until spirit friends can persuade it that it has died and it can go on its way. One that had been well prepared for life after death while in the body, may well be able to negotiate the new awakening with ease and wish to comfort and reassure those it has left behind.

When an Earth body dies there are helpers who will assist the spirit in its transition to the first of the spirit planes. There are six major spirit planes between physical existence and the Ultimate, but as Earth is also sometimes counted as a spirit plane of experience, many people number them as seven—physical existence on Earth is designated as the first plane, the nearest spirit plane to the Earth as the second, and the Ultimate as the seventh. These broad divisions give a rough indication of life beyond the physical. They are not, of course, separate areas of existence, but frequencies or states of being interpenetrating each other as do radio waves. Dense matter is one of the slowest forms of vibration and the grosser the substance the lower its frequency. Fast-moving rays such as X-rays and gamma rays pass effortlessly through matter without necessarily changing its composition, in much the same way as a 'ghost' passes through a wall or door.

It is important to realise that, although the planes are counted as seven in this way, it is only to help visualise existence beyond the physical. They could well be divided into forty-nine, a thousand, or indeed an infinite number, as each provides a wealth of experience in itself. Such are the 'many mansions' waiting to be explored. As the wisdom of the spirit grows, its vibration or frequency becomes finer and higher until it is so fine that it achieves a state of complete harmony with the Ultimate itself.

One is inclined to use the word 'higher', but this does not mean 'above' in the vertical sense. Many people think that the various spirit worlds stretch between the Earth and some remote, unattainable point which they consider to be God. This is not so. All spirit realms interweave so that within and around each person all are present, from the densest to the Godhead itself. It would be more accurate to think in terms of spiritual filters: as a spirit advances it becomes finer and naturally 'percolates' through to a higher vibration. The Godhead, being the finest of all, pervades all.

One day in 1956, the friends were told to expect a 'great teacher' who would want to speak to them in a more serious way. René told them that the light of this spirit was too bright for them, they would have to step back. The reaction of the group was one of awe and puzzlement. They felt rather inadequate to cope with the 'major message' kind of experience. The spirits which had appeared to them so far were from relatively close to the earth. But at Christmas that year Tony first tuned into Helio-Arcanophus.

"Above all it was the aura and the light he emanated that I was aware of; a feeling of immense energy and power and light, yet a *complete* humility". That was Tony's first impression, and today he still experiences H-A in this way. But in those early days he also received an impression of a very tall person, taller than people are today, and slim with aquiline features. He had fair shoulder-length hair parted in the middle and large slanted, very blue eyes, golden skin and high cheek bones. He wore a white girdled robe with a blue cloak and golden sandals, and a golden jewelled chain with a large blue diamond in the centre. A tremendous sense of calm and justice, a 'being-ness' prevailed.

It was as though H-A belonged not only to the planet,

but somehow to the universe beyond. They were impressed not only by what he said, but also his 'emotional
presence'. Indeed, when they began asking questions,
perhaps, a little irreverently, some time after their first
introduction, Dame Nellie Melba came through and said
in a strong Australian accent that she would "take my
brolly to the lot of you, the way you talk disrespectful to
H-A. If you could only see who you are talking to."

The first time he spoke it was with great feeling. He told
the group, through Tony, that he had come not to give
them evidence, not to satisfy their questions, but to
give a universal teaching: a teaching of light and love. This
was his task. He had come not because his teaching was
necessarily right and anyone else's wrong, but because his
was an aspect of the truth that he felt was necessary for
certain spirits on this planet at this time, in order to find
fulfilment and understanding. "I cannot make you take it
down for me," he said, "but I ask you to do so. There is
no reward, and there will be people who say 'So what?
Who do you think you are?' In fact it will be hard for you
to deliver this message. But I must ask you if you are
prepared to do this. I ask you three times, in accordance
with the law of three requests."

The group was stunned. Jackie found herself saying yes.
H-A asked them to take up writing equipment and said
that each time he came through he would tell them so
much. During this first appearance he told them of a place
which existed many thousands of years ago in which there
was light, but the light was put out by the forces of
darkness. That light had to be rekindled. He talked about
the beginning of the Earth and how the Earth was formed.
He told them of old civilisations before the time of
Atlantis.

For an ordinary group of people in their early twenties,
leading ordinary lives, who had never heard of spiritual
teachers like Madame Blavatsky, Rudolf Steiner or Alice
Bailey, the effect of this philosophy pouring through was

mind-blowing. When they asked their teacher, "Who are you?", he replied,

> *I am what I am, no more no less.* I am part of the universal divinity, as you are part of the universal divinity. I see the same truth as you see, but perhaps I see it in a slightly broader perspective. If I could convey to you accurately the picture as I see it, then you would be where I am, beyond the need of all the self discovery that you are going through at the present time. No man in a physical shell can truly know what lies beyond that which he is capable of understanding at any one time. And yet that which he is capable of understanding at any one time can change in itself. Today he will understand what he did not understand yesterday.
>
> That is who I am. That is where I am and how I am. I am love, I am light. But are we not all love and light? I am that which I hope can help you to discover a little more light within yourselves. If I can help you to discover that light, then we are both enlightened. For as you benefit and learn, I benefit and learn. I have come from beyond the confines of the Earth to try to help Earth in its present stage of evolution. I am part of Earth in its present stage of evolution. It is a difficult question you ask, for I can only truly answer that if you could see the question and answer as I do, then you would not be asking the question. I am not attempting to play spiritual conundrums with you, but you must accept that I want to give you an answer that has sufficient depth for you to understand, without first of all trying to see me as I am not, or making me what you would like me to be.

H-A said that names did not matter because names are limiting. Sensitives tune into a level of consciousness. If it is appropriate for a guide to be recognised as a Red Indian called White Feather for a particular group, then fine, the guide is quite happy to be acknowledged as a Red Indian, even though that vibration will represent only one of his life experiences. He told them, however, that if they needed something to know him by, they should call him Helio-Arcanophus, meaning High Priest of the Sun. He explained that this was a title by which he was known when incarnate on the continent of Atlantis.

H-A made no dramatic second appearance. He came through fairly frequently, two or three times a week. He would slip in when the group sat quietly together. The longest trance was an hour and three-quarters, which is a long time to be 'under'. They began to invite others to hear him: one or two at first, like Norman Blunsden, an astrologer, and Muriel Graves, a school teacher, who later worked as a sensitive. H-A invited questions and they asked about UFOs, death, reincarnation, the world.

Originally Tony tuned into H-A by completely relaxing his body and visualising H-A, the feeling he carried. As he relaxed more and more, he could feel H-A coming closer and closer until they seemed to merge together. Later, if there were unpleasant influences around or he was too nervous to relax in front of two or three hundred people, some sort of instinct guided him to reach H-A's level by *drawing in* energy, as though "blowing up the aura". He then visualised H-A and when he felt a 'signal' above him, he literally ejected out of his body and reached up towards H-A. One part of him had faith that he could achieve certain levels of consciousness by activating himself to do so. If he was meant to be the person through whom the teaching came, then he felt he would be given help and protection. But although this method gives Tony more control, H-A did once 'tick him off', because it is far more exhausting.

Although not always conscious of what H-A was saying, particularly in the early days, he was always aware of his moods. "I could feel sadness or heaviness and would ask the others when I woke up what had been the problem. Or I could feel a lot of jubilation to do with whatever came forth. Sometimes he used to come through with such a force I found it almost physically shattering and I was completely exhausted."

For Tony just the experience of doing a trance like this, especially some of the earlier ones, was like being blown apart. "Even now when I bring through Helio-Arcanophus I am on a high for four or five hours. I can remember in the early days never being able to sleep after a trance. My whole metabolism quickened and when I came out I felt my perception was so acute, my reactions were two or three times faster than usual. I have never taken hallucinogenic drugs of any nature and I wouldn't, but I imagine it could be something like that. I don't think necessarily that is a bonus, however. As with drugs, when you come down you are much worse off. I would sometimes be depressed after that, but I have learned how to cope with this over the years and to adjust the subtle bodies, so the effect isn't quite the same."

Tuning into H-A was a feeling so unique it was impossible to find words to describe it, says Tony. At the same time there was always an element of fear. Fear not so much of anything difficult happening, but of not picking anything up. "Most people think that if a sensitive relaxes to pick up a spirit it automatically happens. It is like tuning into a radio station," says Tony, "but more difficult because there is no dial. Tuning in with your mind is far more subtle—it is not like tuning into Radio I!" There have been times, though rare, when H-A has simply not been there. There was also the constant worry: was what he was picking up genuine? And if so, what was it? "Even my scanty knowledge of the Bible covered false prophets. I was scared about the responsibility of what I was doing. It didn't take long to see the effect on the people around me of those early trances. They were awestruck. This worried me. If I was being used as a medium, as a false prophet, and it was totally wrong, this was a terrible thing, even if it was unwittingly done. Did I go on or just stop? Whom could I go to for help?"

For a man who was practical and logical, who could see the potential weaknesses and flaws in what he was doing, it was an enormous struggle. Tony admits now that this identity crisis, this need to be critical of himself, has always kept him one step back, even to the detriment of progress in the work. Yet, on reflection, it is Tony's own cynicism that has probably been healthy for all who came to be involved. He has never lived in a fool's paradise of illusion, the paramount danger of this kind of experience. And alongside the scepticism came a healthy curiosity to see what lay ahead.

Chapter Two

The Atlanteans

Flowing from Helio-Arcanophus, through Tony Neate, was a wealth of esoteric information, including elements of prophecy. What, the friends wondered, were they to do with it all? Tony for the moment had vowed that he would not read any books on the subject in case he might influence the lectures coming through him. Jackie and others, however, had made investigations and were impressed to discover that this type of teaching bore some relationship to existing spiritual philosophies like Anthroposophy and Theosophy.

Jackie, who at that time was working as a case worker for the Officers' Association of the British Legion—in Belgrave Square—noticed one day, in passing, the Marylebone Spiritual Association (MSA) at number 33 (now the Spiritualist Association of Great Britain). She was keen they should go there. The Association had 10,000 books. Perhaps they could find out what they were doing. So the friends began to attend a regular discussion group at the MSA, which was interesting, but did offer one particularly sobering challenge. Tony recounts how in the basement canteen of the Association, he met during their first afternoon, three people who claimed to be Jesus Christ! "It was one of the most formative things that happened to me", he says. "It really pointed out the dangers of illusion."

At the MSA they met Major Norman Leith Hay Clark.

He was a Council member of the Association, an enthusiast in psychic matters of the old school; one of the pioneers of the 1930s who had slept in the pyramids in Egypt to further his researches and loved to give talks about theories in dispute. They told the Major about their discarnate guide Helio-Arcanophus, and asked him where they might go for help and advice. In reply he invited them for an evening at his South Kensington flat, where Tony did a trance and the Major himself was able to talk to H-A.

His reaction was immediate; he was impressed. A teaching of this quality was only tackled by a guide or spirit from one of the higher planes. The group, he felt sure, had stumbled on something important. "Why don't you start your own group?" he suggested. "I'll be the first member." And he gave them their first £5 subscription, which was a generous sum of money in those days. Later Helio-Arcanophus declared that if this was what they wanted to do, he was perfectly happy to be the founder of a society which could correlate his teachings. "He warned us, though, that if we did this, it would change the course of our lives," says Tony. "And by golly, it did."

The Atlanteans society was born in London at 10.40 pm on 11 April 1957. The sun was in Aries, representing a fiery, pioneering determined and energetic impulse. Sagittarius was rising, with Uranus exactly trine to it, implying positive aspirations towards higher learning and the ability to view old problems through new perspectives. In those heady days it was fashionable to give such groups grandiose names like 'The Universal This' or 'The Ultimate That'. The friends, however, decided to avoid that trap.

There are various recognisable spiritual vibrations: Buddhic, Taoist or Christian, for example. H-A's philosophy quite definitely operated on a certain vibration or state of consciousness, which they recognised fairly soon.

It was clearly different from, say, the Egyptian vibration, which they also tuned into through the Pharaoh Akhnaton, or the Buddhic vibration. It was much closer to what could loosely be called the 'Christ' vibration, which they had experienced on occasions.

H-A's wavelength was a distinct, very gentle, very subtle level of energy with a marked yet gentle humour. Helio-Arcanophus was connected with Atlantis and the name Atlanteans sounded sufficiently mundane, although it also embodied that level of understanding and energy. So, Atlanteans it was. H-A suggested they take the symbol of Uranus to represent the society. Uranus rules the sign of Aquarius, the coming solar age.

The original four friends became the founder members: Edwin Naylor, who died in 1962, Jackie, Tony and Mary Prestage. Mary left soon afterwards because she realised she could not make the kind of serious commitment that this would eventually prove to demand. No-one at that stage had any idea the society would evolve into what it has become today. Shortly afterwards Jackie and Tony moved into a flat in Kensington, where meetings with H-A were opened to the public and talks arranged on all kinds of subjects related to the teachings.

A small group met once a week. People heard about them and came along. Yet those early days were problematical in some ways. People did not accept these things as easily as they do now. One evening, for example, three 'rather menacing' young men came to the meeting. During the trance talk given by H-A through Tony, they began to provoke H-A, picking on everything he said. "I wasn't aware," says Tony, "but apparently H-A handled them magnificently with love and tolerance. H-A won't argue, he was not trying to prove he was right." The men, it turned out, were Scientologists. One of them, Colin Bennett, who worked for the British Council, felt so embarrassed afterwards that he left Scientology and join-

ed the Atlanteans, staying for about eight years. It cost
him considerable personal pain because he was pressuris-
ed by his former associates for many years.

Yet life with H-A had its endearing moments. One evening four friends were driving back from a meeting in
Lincoln, all very tired. Quite suddenly Jackie, who was
sitting in the front passenger seat, saw that Tony was
driving at 70 mph with his head forward and his eyes
closed. He looked asleep but nonetheless was dipping the
lights and moving the wheel. She was on the verge of
panic when H-A's voice came through: "Don't worry, my
dears, I'm in charge of the situation. We're enjoying this",
he went on. "Please don't bring him round." The voice
continued to command: "I must do this . . .and this. . . "
for eight minutes or so, until finally H-A said, "You'd
better ease him gentle back into his body now!" Back to
himself, Tony refused to believe he had not been driving.
But no, he was told firmly, H-A had been driving.

On another occasion, during a talk in a public hall, Tony
was in trance. Completely unconscious of his physical
body, he was walking backwards and forwards across the
platform, until his feet became perilously poised over the
edge. While the people in the first six rows sat up in tension, two moved forward to catch him as he hung in
balance. "Didn't you trust me?" H-A said later, with his
usual gentle humour.

The society's membership grew. Meetings were held in
Caxton Hall and the London Vegetarian Society headquarters in Marloes Road, Kensington. In the late 1950s
the ideas of psychic phenomena caught the imagination
of a number of people, including a young Welsh actor,
Henley Thomas. Henley was born in Cardiganshire, but
moved to London as a young man to train as a
draughtsman. There, through a local church drama group,
he became interested in the theatre, and at the age of
twenty-four went to RADA. At the same time he was
becoming interested 'in a general way' in psychic and

spiritual things, although for Henley then it was something "one didn't talk about too loudly. You were still looked upon as a bit weird if you went deeper than reading palms or astrology." A girlfriend suggested they go to a talk given by the Atlanteans at Caxton Hall. Henley was then twenty-eight.

"I didn't know what to expect. Tony was doing a trance lecture and I listened feeling rather embarrassed; it was all so new. But it impressed me." After the talk, Henley met some of the Atlanteans, Tony amongst them. He bought the society's book *Daughter of Atlantis* about H-A's life in Atlantis, published in 1958. H-A had given the story and Jackie had filled in the details through far memory. "Reading the book I felt something quite deeply", says Henley. "It all seemed familiar. It was drawing me towards it. It jogged memories, but I couldn't fix anything." The teachings themselves, now being produced by the society in booklet form, impressed him as a philosophy that looked at life in the present day, that was relevant for now.

From them on Henley went regularly to the public meetings. He joined the Atlanteans in 1959 and became actively involved, not within the inner core, but helping to run the society by working in the office. Always a comprehensive philosophy, out of the teachings had evolved a system of meditation and a unique method of healing, based on knowledge from Atlantis. The Atlanteans had become active in both these fields and Henley was interested in developing as a sensitive and healer. Very early on he knew that this was the right spiritual path for him.

The acknowledged leader and motivator of the society was Jackie, an exceptionally gifted psychic with a wide knowledge of the esoteric field. Along with Tony and two or three others, she too was now 'taking H-A', who was coming through a great deal at that time, not only for public talks, but also privately. Although members themselves could converse with H-A fairly regularly to ask about their own development, it was Jackie or Tony and one or two core members who taught people like Henley who were eager to learn.

An interesting characteristic of Atlantean methods is that they are beautifully safe and direct. H-A did not give details. He would give the fundamentals, the broad outline, and it was up to the group to expand and teach. Jackie in particular had the kind of versatile and imaginative mind that could expound in more detail. As Tony says, when you establish a group you have the inspiration from above, but as you begin to work and think and write together, you are in any case picking up more through group inspiration.

H-A, then, brought through a method or technique for healing that was good and safe, which produced optimum effects with as few problems as possible to the healer. The principle was simple, but like all simple things it is only with practice and experience and understanding that full benefit can be gained. The Atlantean healer learned to use his mind as a transformer for the cosmic forces that exist throughout the universe. Today the healing requires that the healer should delve deeply into himself, to become aware of his own psychological process. But in those early days the techniques asked less for wholeness within the healer himself, than for an understanding of the harnessing and discipline of thought. The positive application of thought, said H-A, could help redress the imbalances that cause disease, both mental and physical.

The power of thought is infinite; indeed, it could be regarded as the energy of the universe. The Godhead, all the different forms of evolution, the people existing in the various solar systems, the animals, physical matter throughout the cosmos, all these in their infinity owe their very existence to the power of thought.

Every aspect of human life is the result of thought:

philosophy, art, science, all forms of invention, healing and, indeed, life itself, for we are all thoughts of God. The Godhead itself is but supreme and infinite thought or intelligence. Thought influences your life from birth to death. There are many things in the world today that could be achieved by the power of thought if man only knew how to use this great gift.

Every human being is capable of using thought positively to a greater or lesser extent, the only limiting factors being those of ability, innate wisdom or evolution and knowledge of how to use that thought power. In other words, nothing and no one else can limit you except yourself and your own attitudes of mind. The universe itself is thought existing on many different levels, from the finest to the densest; the amount of the universe you can conceive is infinite in so far as you are able to broaden your thought to accept, understand and comprehend it. The extent to which the power of thought can be harnessed is limitless.

At various times through history, there has been a great deal of nonsense talked about the secrets of the universe. These are not petty rituals, nor are they some mysterious knowledge only attainable by a few. The secret of the universe is the power of thought. If it were not for the power of thought none of you would be reading this book. You could not eat, drink, sleep or walk. The majority of diseases of the body and the mind and, in fact, the majority of all Earth problems today are due to the misuse of thought force, for this is negative power and as such becomes just as great a potential force as the more positive thought force.

So much can be achieved by the power of thought. There is healing to help all forms of life and forces to be released which can assist in bringing a balance to the planet, so that all beings can learn to express themselves with love, tolerance, humility and understanding towards their fellow beings. One has to think clearly and strongly and direct one's thought positively, that is *with* the flow of the cosmos.

So great is the power of thought that it could be used to quell riots and disturbances, it could be used to stop a war; but it must always be sent in the right direction and not used for evil or selfish purposes. It must never be used to over-ride a fellow being or even a creature from another form of evolution. He who feels tempted to send out negative thoughts with intent to harm another—thoughts that work against the flow of the cosmos—will draw the full force of the law of rebound upon himself. Jesus understood this in all its depths; he said simply, "As ye sow, so shall ye reap."

Those entrusted with the gift of using this thought-force must always recognise the Ultimate with humility and obedience. Thought power can destroy; when wrongly used it can cause psychosomatic disorders, breakdowns and many mental illnesses. The other edge of that sword must be used, the side which builds, mends and puts matters right.

A healer who is capable of transmitting a certain form of healing energy can indeed effect great physical changes such as the dispersion of unwanted tissue and the healing of bone conditions. Since the whole basis of Atlantean healing is thought there is no need for the healers to touch their patients at all; any movements made with their hands are only done as a form of directive for their power and to aid them psychologically in concentrating their thought-force to the best of their ability.

Every spirit in the human body has an aura. It is an etheric substance emanating from the spirit that surrounds the physical shell and acts as a case or covering for it, thus protecting it from all cosmic forces. If the physical body, its counterpart the etheric body, and its other subtle bodies had not this protective robe or force-field, they would be open to influence of all natures and would certainly not survive. The human aura can be opened voluntarily or involuntarily and anyone aware of this can learn to keep his own aura well closed.

When a person's aura is open all substances of a malevolent nature may enter. A sudden physical strain or jerk can serve to cause an opening, such as in the case of an accident where a leg is broken or flesh injuries sustained. Cases of disease involving viruses or germs can soon be brought under control by realigning the physical and etheric bodies and sealing the aura, for such particles of life cannot exist unless they breathe from the ether; in fact, they live on the impurities in the ether. It is also possible to cleanse the aura and the body to a certain extent by the use of a cleansing ray.

Medical science has found that the use of bandages and artificial forms of sterilisation is effective in cases of surface wounds, inasmuch as they give the aura time to adjust itself while the natural healing processes take their course. By the use of the power of thought the Atlantean healer seals the aura in the affected places, so that the resident impurities will die from lack of nourishment and can be dispersed in the normal manner. This speeds up the healing process.

All diseases are caused by imbalances which create a maladjustment between the physical body, the subtle bodies and the spirit and until these are brought into balance and alignment the physical condition will not improve. If the sufferer is a strong willed person he may be able, with assistance from his spirit, to put right the maladjustment, but in most cases the services of a healer will greatly speed up this rebalancing process.

As for diagnosis: legally, the layman is precluded from making a medical diagnosis, which is indeed a good thing. So, in observance of the law, Atlantean healers make a point of not telling their patients what they feel is wrong. However, as the healer becomes more sensitive, more aware of the subtler energies, he is often able to delve down to the primary cause of the trouble and offer a few tentative suggestions that could help the patient to rid himself of his problem in the ordinary course of life. The advice might be for more rest, or a regulated diet, or an immediate visit to a physician; or, in some instances, the healer is able to offer counselling where a deeper problem may be a contributing factor.

There are no intermediaries in Atlantean healing, no guides, spirits or deceased doctors that take possession of the healers and do their work for them. All is carried out in full consciousness, for this is the age of the mind when man must learn to be responsible for his thought and actions. Leaning on the discarnate is helping neither them nor him. A healer, however, will always ask for inspiration from the powers that be and healing is offered with the proviso 'If it be Thy will.'

It is possible to bring about miracle cures but great power would have to pass through the healer and the amount of power any healer can take at any one particular time is dependent on many factors. The physical body needs to be trained to take a fine vibration and few people today are prepared to put themselves out sufficiently to achieve the necessary balance between spirit and body to take such power. Although we speak of a healer who cures, what the healer is actually doing is assisting the patient to cure himself. A healer is a person who is a suitable channel for a certain type of power which, when directed by thought to the etheric body of a sufferer, aids the patient's own spirit to make the necessary adjustment.

Healing was a regular part of the society's public meetings, and later there were separate special healing evenings for working on individuals, and also for absent healing. Since Atlantean healing uses the power of thought, time and space are not barriers to effective work. Absent healing, by picturing someone mentally or tuning into their vibration, can be equally effective and sometimes more so.

H-A said almost anyone can learn to heal, although obviously some are better at it than others. It is a question of dedication, discipline and thought control and, further, whether it is part of the karmic pattern of this life to heal. If a member was really interested to learn and the core group felt him to be rightly motivated, they would teach him the techniques. If, however, someone was experiencing difficulties in his own life and feeling out of balance, he was advised that this was not a good time to learn to heal. On the other hand, if the problem was a minor one, learning to heal could often help the healer and clear up his own physical problem as a result of the energy flow.

By 1959 Jackie and Tony, who were convinced that their purpose in coming together was to create the Atlanteans, felt their marriage was no longer appropriate, and mutually agreed to divorce. Jackie continued to be the society's charismatic leader. In 1960 Tony met and married Ann Dowdall, a talented and dedicated singer, who had already made a name for herself. As an 'over-serious' adolescent who 'perhaps grew up too quickly', in her late teens Ann was already interested in spiritual philosophy and looking for a 'spiritual home'. Her mother had died when Ann was ten, bringing to an abrupt halt a promising dancing career, alongside Beryl Grey and Gillian Lynne. At eighteen she went to the Royal College of Music to study piano and after three years decided to take up singing professionally. She was in the first production of Purcell's "Dido and Aeneas" at the original Mermaid Theatre, built by Sir Bernard Miles in his own garden.

At thirty-one Ann was unmarried but sufficiently secure within herself to accept that this might be permanent. Disharmony was so distasteful to her that she knew she could never marry for security. But no sooner the acceptance than the situation changed. Her younger sister Sally, who followed in her footsteps at the Royal College of Music, told her about a singer she had met at college who was psychic and lived with some people who ran a small society called the Atlanteans. This singer was Jackie.

Sally brought home their booklets for Ann to read. "I was staggered because everything I read seemed to answer the questions that had been in me for so long," she recalls. "It rang bells for me in every direction. It was saying what I had always felt."

Fascinated and intrigued, Ann attended an Atlantean public lecture at the Vegetarian Society. It was on astrology. The following week she returned, this time to hear a trance-talk by H-A. She also met Tony. "Before I met them my sister had said there was one man called Tony amongst the group who she thought would be a nice partner for me. That was enough to make me go mentally in the opposite direction!" But within five months Tony and Ann were married. Ann had found not only her spiritual home, but her husband as well.

She felt at home with these people. She could discuss things she had always longed to be able to express. She had never thought of herself as a healer, but when it was suggested to her she thought it a wonderful idea. If the group thought she had the ability then she would love to be able to try. She smiles when she remembers her first experience of healing. The group had decided to go to Bournemouth to see a girl who was very ill. "It was a very immature way of going about it, but in our enthusiasm about ten of us gave her power. We must have totally embarrassed the poor girl. Needless to say no great healing took place, but fortunately she survived!"

Where the teachings were concerned the Atlanteans in some ways had no conception of what they held. In the early days it was the phenomenon of it all that was exciting. Here they were a small, pioneering group, to whom people—some pretty strange—were intuitively drawn. The teaching found its mark quickly, the social barriers came down and all kinds of different people were able to share their experiences freely. This, in part, was what appealed to Patricia Thomas. As an actress she enjoyed the camaraderie of the theatre and she found that this same camaraderie existed in the Atlanteans too, because everyone shared a common philosophy. Tricia sensed an easy identification with people as though from aeons gone by, which somehow added an extra dimension.

Tricia was introduced to the society in 1960 just before her marriage to Henley. The two had met while performing in *A Midsummer Night's Dream* at Manchester Library Theatre. When Henley first told her, cautiously in case it frightened her away, that in another part of his life he was a sensitive and healer, she totally accepted the fact and, what is more, was interested. When the Thomases came to London he introduced her to the rest of the Atlanteans—"A varied bunch," she remembers. "One or two a little bit daunting, because they existed on a level I didn't, but very nice and normal. It was the simplicity that made me warm to them."

As Henley's wife, Tricia felt a sense of privilege. She could penetrate the aura of the society without, just then, taking part in the psychic activities. "People talked in front of me and it sifted down to the right level for me." She was happy listening and learning, but it was not until five years later, partly due to family and work, that she commenced any psychic training. Nevertheless, Tricia too felt she had 'come home'. Like Henley she became tirelessly involved in the practical side of the society, especially when in 1962 the Atlanteans bought, through membership donations, their first headquarters. Gradually they were coming together as a group with a real foundation.

The first two floors of 45 Earls Court Road were in a messy state. It took much hard work and enthusiasm to make the building habitable. Unsuitable for large public meetings, it was ideal for social gatherings and healing sessions; there were also a library and an office. "We made it more or less into a club," says Tricia. "In a minute space we built a kitchenette and created a bar counter next to the loo." Yet this excruciatingly small space became a veritable hive of activity.

Healing took place upstairs; eggs on toast and deep

philosophical conversations were provided downstairs. They were all extremely serious, but on another level, says Tricia, they had to laugh at themselves. Anyone was free to express whatever he wished and the 'club' was a natural attraction for many lonely people, the so-called misfits, who were attracted to the feeling of the place as well as to the philosophy. Tricia remembers "our first transvestite—such a tortured man, so gentle. With us he thought he could relax and the clothing became more and more weird. Again it was a forerunner of the counselling side of the work, if you like. You learned that you cannot judge people on the surface level."

There were many visitors, some who came to 'suss them out'. One came with a young girl and asked them to diagnose what was wrong with her. Very inexperienced in those days they described a patch on one of her lungs and pointed to the place—they would never diagnose today since it is against the law to do so. Whereupon an X-ray was produced by the visitors proving that they were exactly correct. There were also many personal challenges, a constant testing of their own understanding. As Henley says, "It caused me a lot of personal headaches and traumas. It made me look at myself deeply. Was I really worthy of all this, bringing through healing and having such close contact with someone I believed to be of a very high evolution?"

The society at no time intended to 'go public' to any large extent. In addition to Tony's residual reticence, they all had day-to-day jobs and a living to earn. The member-ship remained constant; people came and went. As some members left others took their place; it was like a breathing in and out. Another long-time and current member of the society Joyce Mitchell arrived in the 1960s. She had seen an advertisement for a Caxton Hall lecture and a strong feeling swept through her that she must make contact. She ran the society's canteen for many years and later became Chairman of The Atlanteans Main Council.

Helio-Arcanophus appeared less than in the first years. As well as trance talks by Tony, the society's Sunday evening lectures covered associated subjects, such as astrology, for example, or Rudolf Steiner's philosophy, with invited speakers. By this time the Atlantean magazine was flourishing and four or five branches of the society had been set up in other parts of the country, by people deeply involved in the inner teachings, rather than structured and organised by headquarters. Each branch held weekly meetings and most offered meditation and other activities to help people to greater understanding of themselves.

In 1968 Tony and Ann moved to Ealing. 45 Earls Court Road was sold and a small office purchased at Hanger Lane. Lectures continued in the Friends Meeting House in Ealing where Patricia and Henley also decided to move. Imperceptibly the society was evolving as the people involved were themselves growing and changing.

Chapter Three

Psychic in Safety

Much of the teaching of Helio-Arcanophus emerged in answer to questions. What made it so unique was the wide area it covered: philosophy, prophecy, indications for a way of life for today, historical information. It also encompassed deeply occult and esoteric subjects such as the principles of cosmic law and the true meaning of the life of Christ. Above all, H-A taught the Atlanteans the mechanics of psychism, something which was seriously lacking in those days. Many people used their psychic ability and experienced phenomena, but few understood how to handle the energies with safety.

There are dangers involved in psychic development. When H-A first explained psychic energy and taught the group how to use it in a disciplined way, he made it clear that man is responsible for the right use of this energy. One of the most frequent hazards for example, is when a sensitive goes out of his body 'by mistake'. This sometimes happens to Tony Neate, but more often than not he knows how to control the situation and bring himself back. Even so, there have been mishaps. On one occasion he was map-reading in the car sitting next to Ann who was driving. The car suddenly took off over a hump in the road and Tony shot out of his body. He remained half-in and half-out, unable to come back squarely. Fortunately he was able to explain to Ann what had happened, and she stopped the car to give him healing and bring him back into alignment.

Yet there are people in psychic development circles, beginning to develop as mediums or healers, who have not been taught psychic disciplines or how to cope with this kind of eventuality.

On one occasion, for example members of the Atlanteans met two girls at the Festival of Mind, Body and Spirit in London. After three months of instruction they had been assured they were developed mediums, yet both had slipped out of their bodies without realising what had happened. Both were on the verge of a nervous breakdown. When they were 'put back' through healing their problems were resolved.

It is worth observing here that when a sensitive is out of body in a trance he should never be touched. Once when a cat jumped on to Tony's knee and dug his claws in, Tony found himself lying on the floor doubled up in pain, totally disoriented and feeling as though he had been kicked in the stomach. He had been jolted back into his body, and it took him fifteen minutes to recover. The spirit is joined to the body in two places: at the head and the solar plexus. If someone astrally projects and then comes back too quickly, one or both of these centres will be in a state of shock.

Conscious astral projection like this must not be confused with astral experience during sleep. Experience of other dimensions during sleep is an involuntary projection of the spirit onto the inner planes for the purpose of learning or helping in one way or another. It is involuntary in the sense that the mind does not consciously cause the projection. As the spirit is involved, the ethics concerned originate from the inner rather than the surface conscience and will be determined by the evolutionary state of the spirit. These experiences usually have a feeling of clarity and logic although they may not be strictly logical by Earth standards, coming from a dimension for which there are no terms of reference in Earth language.

It is up to the individual to learn to distinguish between astral experience and dreams. In dreams the subconscious mind brings forward a set of experiences to the conscious mind, most of which are forgotten when you wake. The subconscious is a vast storehouse, a highly efficient computer that records your every thought, feeling and action, whether good, bad or indifferent. Deeper inner messages from your spirit can surface in dreams, using the symbolic language of imagery from the subconscious and act as clarifying or even healing agents. At other times dreams are concerned with the surface conscience that is related to the conscious mind and influenced by social environment and pressures. Such dreams act as a safety valve for tension and repressions, helping to adjust the mind that has been subjected to frustration or another form of stress.

Sometimes while a person is asleep, his spirit might try to bring something through to the conscious brain in the form of a warning or a communication from another plane. A psychic person will more easily be able to remember this type of precognitive or premonitory 'dream' as the link between his spirit and his conscious mind will be stronger than in other people. However, even this sort of message will have picked up irrelevant detail on its way through the subconscious mind and care must be taken to recognise the significant material if the dreamer wishes to interpret the dream—a valuable adjunct to psychotherapy and counselling. Compared to this, however, the feeling when the spirit returns to the body after visiting other planes during astral experience is unmistakable. The term 'astral' incidentally, is often loosely used to denote all the various inner planes, but strictly speaking it should only apply to the thought planes nearest to the physical world and not to the more spiritual realms.

Conscious astral projection, however, is quite another story and can be dangerous if it is not learned under the guidance of a teacher. The Atlanteans certainly advise against it. One particular event rests clearly in their minds. The group were telephoned by a girl asking for help and advice about a frightening aspect of her astral travelling. Immediately they warned her that there were dangers in her activities, but she assured them that she knew what she was doing. This, in fact, was the first object lesson. According to H-A one of the greatest weaknesses in any psychic work is to say "I know."

The girl told them she had projected from her body and in this state had become aware of a group in Hampstead who were practising black magic. Unfortunately they saw her looking in at them and followed her back on the astral. Some time later these people made physical contact with her and warned her that if she spied on them again they would 'teach her a lesson'. She was so frightened she was unable to go to sleep in case they came after her. Could the Atlanteans help?

H-A consented to protect her providing she stopped astral travelling. If she did so again she would be taking herself outside his protection. She agreed, and three days later called to tell the group that the whole atmosphere had changed: she felt a golden band of protection around her, and it was wonderful. A few days after that, however, because she had never slept so well and was no longer afraid, she decided to take another look. One of the first spirits she met on the astral was a member of this Hampstead group and she fled back to her home with the group chasing closely behind. She flew back into her body and as she did so the group followed, hitting H-A's wall of protection. There was an enormous crash as the whole of the window and the frame hurtled out onto the floor, but she was safe.

From the beginning H-A was extremely practical on how to handle psychism. He imbued the group with a thorough understanding of the laws of the universe, until they knew instinctively how to handle these phenomena. H-A made much of the aura. As explained earlier, every living creature has an aura. It is the psychic force field surrounding the physical and etheric bodies and acts as a protective envelope against the alien elements in the ether. Without this auric barrier the incarnate spirit would be wide open to all kinds of influences that would allow it very little chance to pursue its own evolution.

Few people on Earth today understand how to control their auras. If this ability were more widespread there would not be the disease and mental illness with which the world abounds. The trained, and in some cases, the natural psychic can see the human aura. It will be perceived as a colour or combination of colours, and these give a clue both to the subject's evolution and physical, mental and emotional health.

With practice, however, the student can soon learn auric control. If people who are frightened when psychic experiences confront them could practise a meditative discipline to enable them to feel contained within this natural field of protection, they would find themselves helped enormously. They could then work comfortably within their own spiritual space. The stronger the aura, the stronger the protection and the ultimate balance and health of the individual. Then the sensitive is able to pick up the entity when he chooses and not when the entity decides it wants to communicate through him. The incarnate person should always control the situation.

Alongside his healing techniques H-A presented a system of meditation taught as a discipline as well as a relaxation. The Atlantean approach is a system of simple mental and physical exercises designed to give an awareness and control of the mind, body and nervous system which can help every person in ordinary living and also aid those who have psychic potential to explore it in a disciplined manner. It provides a useful grounding for healing.

In this modern world where the advantages of good discipline and periods of quietness are fast being denied to man, there is a growing need for a form of meditation that is easily adaptable to western requirements and which, at the same time, affords the meditator an opportunity to discover possible channels of self-expression and self-realisation through mental disciplines.

If one has the type of concentration needed to focus on an object and sustain this concentration at will, then one can also utilise the principle to 'collect' oneself either physically or mentally in times of stress or strain. Command of the nervous system can afford control over pain and anxiety: and if, at times of great worry, the mind can be temporarily relieved of its tension by such a form of mental discipline, then the spirit can use the period of respite to get through to the brain the best line of action to take to overcome the problem. The calm afforded by divorcing oneself from a serious problem, even if only for a few minutes, can go a long way towards solving it. These are all things for the ordinary person which have nothing to do with psychism but a great deal to do with self-healing.

Concentration on a given point or object to the exclusion of all other thoughts or sensations can give great control over the body at a purely physical level. Visualisation and creative imagination are other aspects of mental development.

As the methods have evolved the Atlanteans have carefully designed exercises to aid the expansion of consciousness within a disciplined framework, so that the path of self-realisation may unfold for the student, helping him to establish his identity and release his full potential.

Most important, Atlantean meditation recognises that during meditation the chakric centres, the vortices of energy in the subtle bodies, may be activated and the aura opened involuntarily, and for this reason there are in-built precautions against possible psychic difficulties. When a psychic person meditates, he is vulnerable to possible psychic interference and he may also unconsciously astrally project out of his body. Unless he is taught how to control his energies he may have some deeply disturbing experiences. There are people who end up in mental hospitals as a result of undisciplined forms of meditation and psychic work. Many are open psychics who do not know how to discipline their psychic energy.

> When a person is a natural sensitive—that is, mediumistic—he is not always aware of the fact. Many cases of schizophrenia, hallucination and so-called vivid imagination are merely those of sensitives who walk through life with open auras through which penetrate all sorts of other spirit minds. They can even be possessed for periods when they are 'not quite themselves' without the possessor being necessarily of an evil nature. It may be a spirit from the second plane that wishes to communicate something it has learnt or to send a message to a loved one. When a person is receptive he is not only open to good influences, but to all influences; hence the case of brilliant artists and composers who receive much of their inspiration from the 'other side' but whose private lives are often far from inspiring.

As soon as he began to extend his psychic capabilities, Tony realised—less from his own experience than through what happened to other people—that not every spirit entity is pleasant. He understood that there is a distinct and vivid difference between good and evil and that there are definitely malevolent spirits on various levels of evolution. This happens most commonly when the spirit within the body is a young or weak spirit and is influenced by those around it in the spirit world. In such a case the incarnate spirit will pay more attention to an interfering spirit than to the task of controlling its own physical body, and this causes great confusion of mind to the person concerned.

> A weak spirit of this nature can be assisted by being aligned more closely to the physical body so that the two can work in greater harmony away from distracting influences. The spirit will then be able to assume greater control of its body. It is rather like the puppeteer who controls his dolls by pulling strings; if one of those strings snaps then that portion of the puppet to which it is attached will cease to function correctly. If, however, he refastens the string the limb will again respond to his will.

Another typical kind of experience of malevolent spirits is in cases of possession, ranging from the violent elemental type to the more subtle possession by a spirit from a higher plane. When people die they do not necessarily 'see the light' overnight. Discarnate spirits are also learning and experiencing. When, say, a drug addict dies, the spirit does not lose the craving for drugs. Even when discarnate he still wants a 'high'. Because of that need the spirit will attach itself to another individual to possess it and encourage that person—whose own demeanour is inclined that way—to take drugs. A person may become 'hooked', not necessarily for his own need but for the need of this other entity. When a person becomes psychologically negative and lets his own disciplines go, if he is psychic he will draw negative psychic states towards him. Disease, the Atlanteans believe, can be caused by both inner and outer imbalances and it is their ability to see this outside aspect that gives their healing an added dimension.

Cases of possession include lunacy, sex mania, many crimes, fits and violent changes of personality. It is unbalanced thought in its wrong domain. The possessing spirit must be exorcised and sent to its own sphere of evolution. Within a year of his first appearance H-A began to talk about exorcism, mainly because the Atlanteans were being approached for help. Again H-A's techniques in those days were unique and contemporary. At first H-A carried out the work while Tony was in trance, but later this changed and a few of the more experienced healers learned to perform the exorcism under H-A's guidance.

Healing is healing at whatever level you are working. It is the handling of the same cosmic divine energy, but operated according to the level on which the particular problem lies. It has been found from experience that healers fall into certain groups or categories according to their own individual make-up and the way in which they act as channels for the cosmic forces. According to the type of ray produced by each healer, so will he be equipped to deal with, say, a physical case, a psychological case, or a patient who is badly disturbed mentally. Cases of possession must primarily be dealt with by the mental healer.

There is nothing vicious or punishing about the exercise, no banishment, but an expression of divine love, presented in such a way that something not of that love cannot exist in that energy. The situation, however, demands a great deal of the healer. The spirit which is possessing must be helped to find and accept its rightful sphere of evolution and given healing, and the native spirit helped to regain control of its own physical body in true alignment and balance.

When a person has been subjected to the strain of being controlled by an alien entity it will take time to build up both the physical body and the aura after the correct spiritual adjustment has been made. A post-possession case must be watched very carefully and recharged regularly until the native spirit has regained complete control of the situation.

Diseases such as cancer are brought on by friction between the physical and etheric bodies, caused very often by severe emotional stress; here again the physical condition will be greatly helped if this can be understood and alleviated. All cancerous parts have a form of entity of their own and this needs to be removed as part of the healing process. The removal of such an entity is carried out by an experienced mental healer before the application of Atlantean healing. The strength of will and determination of the patient also play an active part here.

Mental healing, which uses a finely concentrated healing love-energy, is now a speciality of the Atlanteans. It is a more complicated and somewhat broader field of work, which deals not only with the physical body and the aura but also with outside entities. No person should be engaged in mental healing unless he has been trained to use his mind in a concentrated way to heal cases and situations where a spirit is either lost, outside its rightful sphere of evolution, or is impinging on the freedom and well-being of another, as a parasite. If this advice is ignored there could be a danger to the healer's own mental balance. It is cosmic law which decrees that if a spirit is exorcised, provided the exorcist is more powerful than the possessor, it must obey and leave its possession. At the same time if the healer is insufficiently trained and experienced to cope with the particular situation, the spirit may leave its possession and attack the healer.

Mental healing is a specialised field and often requires help of an occult nature. The word occult conjures up in many people's minds a confusing and sometimes frightening picture of witchcraft, ritual and black magic. Occult merely means hidden: hidden in the sense, said H-A, that it is so obvious no one can see it! In its purest sense it is a conscious use of thought in the positive handling of universal energies, but only from the highest motivation. It does not require external ritual of any sort, but it does require a deep understanding of cosmic law and must be used only in service to God.

In fact, say the Atlanteans, the master occultist was Christ. His gifts of prophecy, walking on the water, healing and casting out of devils, were part of being a great spiritual teacher. H-A describes those who are concerned with these things as students of the universe, rather than occultists. In the past occult information was passed only to those who had the right spiritual perception of how to use the energies, because playing around with such forces can cause damage to others as well as to the practitioner himself.

Occultism is knowledge of the secret wisdom by which the universe and the spirit worlds exist, used for the benefit of others. To anyone who wishes to know more about advanced occult matters I would say: do not seek them out or touch them unless you are under the care and protection of an instructor who knows what he is doing. By playing with fire you are liable to unleash powers on yourself which you are not equipped to control. To be an occultist should but does not necessarily imply spirituality, and there are many pitfalls if you misuse your knowledge for personal power or gain. It is when it is used in this way, for ego reasons and self-agrandisement, that it becomes black magic for it then transgresses cosmic law and will, in due course, rebound on the practitioner.

Many people of apparently strong character have taken up occult studies on the basis of 'Oh, I can tackle anything, nothing frightens *me*'. Such people are seldom able to progress very far and can end up in mental disarray or with their lives disrupted in some way. Bravery does not enter into it; it is a question of spiritual understanding and the type of mind. A good occult healer must be able to make immediate decisions; a moment's hesitation may lose him his sanity. Perception is essential, and strength of mind, but not forcefulness. A fearless person should not touch these things as he will be easily deceived by those who wish him ill. Perhaps fear is the wrong word—words are so limiting—but certainly utter caution and alertness are needed.

If you are meant to study the occult during this lifetime, you will find that the opportunity will present itself. And when it comes, ask yourself deep down inside, 'Am I *really* equipped to touch these things, or is it merely my curiosity, or vanity.

One of H-A's fundamental lessons concerning psychism and healing was the law of polarity. He impressed on the group that to handle psychism safely this principle must be thoroughly understood.

Indeed it is fundamental to any understanding of the universe. The whole universe is a series of polarities held magnetically in balance. To give just a few examples: You are a spirit in a physical body, experiencing physical, material living through a physical shell. In this particular life you have entered a body that is either male or female, for physical life is maintained between the male and female of a species.

You will also know through scientific research that no person is entirely masculine or entirely feminine, that every person is a mixture of each. The way your physical body is constructed and the way in which your mind triggers your body with its particular evolutionary

history, these two factors come together to create a set
of circumstances that helps to maintain the particular
sex of the body in which you are experiencing life. This
in itself is quite a delicate thing, for if any one person—
let us say a man—were subjected to the wrong type of
influence through psychological pressures he could very
quickly start to incline towards the feminine, and if he
were stimulated by drugs the inclination would increase
and could even manifest physically.

The spirit within your body also has a positive or
negative inclination. When you are incarnate you tend
to think of your spirit as being a complete being, but in
fact not all of your spirit is in your body; there is a
counterpart outside the body that is of the opposite
polarity to the spirit within. Every spirit has a dual
nature, a positive and a negative aspect, but only one
part of this duality experiences within the body while
the other aspect acts as a complement, a balancing
factor, experiencing near it, shaping, helping and
guiding it. This is your higher self with which you seek
to communicate and it in turn acts as a link with the
higher spheres.

The Godhead in its wholeness encompasses both
polarities and a spirit rejoins the Godhead at that
moment in its evolution when both its aspects—positive
and negative—have reached perfect harmony with each
other and are therefore in a state of perfect balance.

The relationship between the spirit, the subtle bodies,
the physical body and the aura that surrounds and
protects the whole, is governed by the balance of the
chakras at various points within the body. These are
vortices of energy linking the many levels of consciousness, the means by which spiritual energies are
translated down to the physical. For anyone to function
perfectly, physically and mentally, the polarity of each
one of those chakras needs to be in balance. In healing
it is best to consider the chakric system as a whole and

to use a general balancing thought that will allow them to rebalance naturally.

Everyone is psychic to a greater or lesser degree and many people have experiences of a psychic nature at one time or another in their lives. In this sixth or psychic sense—which has become rather lost in this modern age of scientific materialism—there is also a polarity. For some people are psychically negative, receptive, mediumistic, while others are psychically positive, such as the healer, the one who uses an outgoing psychic energy, the protector, the transmitter and the occult healer who handles inner and outer forces. This polarity is an important factor in psychic work where mediumistic work should be balanced and protected by someone working on a positive wavelength, so that the energies are the best for the medium to work in safely.

For example, when a spirit announces itself through a medium the trained positive will 'challenge' that spirit. When correctly applied it is the cosmic law of challenge which decrees that the spirit should show its 'light' either psychically or physically which will give a clue to what it is and where it comes from. A spirit showing a blue, silver, gold or white light will be quite advanced, while a spirit that does not answer the challenge will disappear: the medium will falter and even stop, complaining that the vibration is not right.

If a psychic is fundamentally 'negative' and a good receiver—clairvoyant perhaps—he may not feel an easy energy flow when he tries to heal. Another who is basically 'positive' may have a strong flow of power for healing but will often find it difficult to see clairvoyantly. To illustrate this, a friend of the society has been a healer for some years with good results, but she secretly worried because she could not 'see' psychically. Once she understood the principle of positive and negative psychism, she realised she was obviously working on the

positive polarity. Just having that knowledge revolution-
ised her life. She was healing intuitively and now accepted
that seeing clairvoyantly no longer mattered. She could
accept herself as she was. It was á simple but profound
realisation.

Although it is usual for a psychic to major in one polarity, it is wise for him also to nurture the other side of his
psychic nature, to experience the opposite polarity as a
counter-balance. Many well-known psychics have
encountered problems when they are over-developed in
one side of their psyche. Either way, when a psychic
develops, the metabolism quickens and great care is
needed to maintain balance on all levels of being, physical,
emotional, mental, psychic, and spiritual. "I have
developed myself as a healer as well as a medium" says
Tony. "This has been a vital aspect of my psychic life and
has enabled me to keep in balance."

In the early days of the society there were certainly
dangers in their psychic work and the macabre side
manifested much more. "When you are launched on an
esoteric wavelength which, especially in those days few
people took seriously, and you are working for light,"
continues Tony, "conversely, you attract the shadow side.
We found ourselves visited by all sorts of wierdos and
cranks such as men who claimed to be from outer space!
They were obviously psychological misfits but quite
frightening to us at the time."

As H-A has already made clear, psychism is neither
good nor bad. It is intention that determines what it is.
Energy can be used for good but also for negative purposes. The culprit is often the ego. A story to illustrate
this, and to emphasise the importance of protection, con-
cerns a counsellor who also uses herbs for healing. Today
she lives happily in a beautiful house with a walled herb
garden. But life was not always so idyllic.

The group knew she had met and befriended a woman
who was extremely psychic, but a year after this she

telephoned to say she was in serious trouble. The atmosphere of her home had completely changed, awful things were happening and there were spirits around in almost physical presence. The situation was such that she had gone to live with her psychic friend, but everyone in that house quarrelled all the time. She was unhappy and, what is more, was doing all the woman's chores. Yet her friend was so psychic. . . .

Over the telephone they asked if she was challenging the spirit when her friend went into trance. Was she making sure she was well protected? "But she is doing it all the time," was the reply. When they asked the psychic herself if she had her own ways of protection and challenging, she was defensive. "My guides are fine", she said. "I'm protected." A medium who is picking up constantly is a totally open psychic and, uncontrolled in this way, can play havoc with other people's lives. Such a person can galvanise a disturbed atmosphere from the past which has been allowed to rest until it comes to life again through a situation like this. This particular psychic woman was being used by entities and had upset the energies in Mary's home.

The problem is the ego, the side of us that thinks it knows best. If the ego demands it, the entities will simply start to use it. By bringing through fantastic information it makes the psychic unwary of what can happen. Through being so open and trusting—and flattered—gradually the wrong sort of entity can use that medium. The Atlanteans spent a whole day cleansing, clearing and rebalancing their friend's house and garden. They taught her how to keep her aura closed and the difficulties ceased immediately.

After years of working with and understanding how to draw and send out energies, the Atlanteans have been through the 'nitty gritty' in the psychic world. Today they accept their responsibility to pass on that knowledge, to help the many people who are now becoming involved in psychism to understand it and how it relates to inner growth. It is vital, they feel, that those with a natural gift should know what they are dealing with; or what to do if something psychic crops up in life that makes them feel afraid and unsure. Someone who innocently uses a pack of tarot cards may unlock doors and be confronted with experiences they cannot handle. People should be aware of the pitfalls and how to avoid them.

In the early days the four friends were not consciously spiritually motivated; their investigations arose out of a natural curiosity concerning psychic phenomena. Today there are countless people at this same stage, undefended against the forces they are contacting. The Atlanteans feel there is a real need to teach people so that they understand the pitfalls and the laws involved, and thereby ensure that the psychic is experienced in the best and safest way. Above all, they should realise that developed on its own it can be dangerous and unbalancing. As the friends were soon to discover for themselves, although psychic awareness is a valuable asset in understanding spiritual mysteries, it is only part of the process of growth towards deeper spiritual understanding. Indeed, psychic development needs to be contained wholly within the path of spiritual growth, used as a tool and not an end in itself.

PART TWO

Towards the Spiritual

Tony and Ann Neate

Chapter Four

Symbols of Change

The Atlanteans is a society which exists on many levels. It offers a philosophy, a way of life, an understanding of the Godhead; and it offers healing which extends beyond the physical to encompass the mental, the spiritual, the etheric and the elemental. Its occult work extends beyond the single individual to helping national and worldwide conditions. This help is always extended in a gentle way, for in following the path of light they can only defend, never attack, and they can only offer love, compassion and understanding. This is an example of the dual nature of the occult; the power of the true occult healer on the path of light contains a great force and yet this must be applied only to influence through the balancing of energies with light and love and never to enforce.

Early in his life David Furlong knew he wanted to become involved in healing, but on a wider scale than just working with individuals. His vision was to try to bring healing and balance to the difficult situations that were continually erupting on the planet. Brought up as a Christian Scientist—a religion with a strong emphasis on healing through the power of the mind—David had always accepted that there were forces beyond ordinary physical existence. He soon recognised that a true comprehension of healing at that level required an understanding of the principles and forces which exist in and around the planet, and how those forces which operate at a deeper level could be used for the growth and development of the planet. It was the fact that the Atlanteans were involved with some of the more 'dramatic' aspects of healing that drew him to the society.

When he left school David went to work in the planning department of one of the London borough councils. "The sort of job that requires you to work three hours in an eight-hour day", he admits candidly. The other five hours he spent reading the entire philosophy, occult and metaphysical sections in the local library, building up a fairly clear picture of what he believed and felt to be right. 'By chance' he heard there was to be a talk on the psychic and paranormal given to the local young Conservative group by Joyce Mitchell, who was then chairman of the Main Council. "It touched me quite deeply," says David. "But more than that, I was aware of a definite 'strong presence' around Joyce Mitchell."

Some time later, when he saw an advertisement for the Atlanteans in *Prediction* magazine, he remembered the talk and wrote for particulars of the society. He decided to join. He bought the teaching booklets, plus back-dated copies of The Atlantean magazine, which happened to be on offer at the time. "It was as though I was being spoken to," he says. The philosophy brought together everything he had ever read on these subjects in a clear and coherent way. Above all, David felt that here was a teaching from someone who was a real 'Master', with a profound wisdom, understanding and perception. It resonated within him. In 1968 he went to his first trance lecture at Caxton Hall, given by Tony, on the positive and negative aspects of creation. He was then twenty-two.

In David's view, if the Atlanteans was right for him, and his wife Diane was right for him too, then The Atlanteans had to be right for Diane! Diane, who was brought up as a 'straight' Catholic, was perfectly happy just going to church regularly. She believed "each to his own idea of religion", but certainly did not believe in the psychic.

When she married David in 1969 she went along with his ideas, taking the attitude that "if it makes David happy....", and "it's a fad that will pass." After a year the fad still had not passed, however. The teachings were too deeply ingrained in him. Now he had found something that meant so much to him there was no chance he could give them up. Diane finally accepted that she had two options: either to leave David or go along with him.

In the end, she says, it was a question of "if you can't beat them, join them", so she did, although she did remain aloof for quite some time, as though part of her was saying "this is not for me." They both joined the Bromley branch of the Atlanteans, which ran an absent healing group. There they learned the different healing techniques that had come from headquarters, directly or indirectly through Helio-Arcanophus. A talented clairvoyant, Wyn Ratcliff, also brought through information which gave David in particular encouragement to persevere. He felt sure that the Atlanteans was the right path for him to begin to express whatever it was within him that needed to be expressed. Learning the techniques of healing was a step towards opening that channel.

Some time after David and Diane joined the Bromley branch, H-A asked that the couple should be given more advanced development training. Although from Diane's point of view they were still very much on the fringes of the society, they went regularly to London to train in various kinds of psychic work. This was taught mainly on a one-to-one basis, by those members who had a broad grasp of the force that was coming through H-A. As David points out, however, the main object is to experience these energies, and experience cannot be taught. Various techniques were explored to expand psychic sensitivity. For example, the teacher would provide an object and ask, "what do you sense of it?" Or, "there is a spiritual being behind you, are you aware of it?" and the student would have to tune in in his own way.

One particular experience of David's was quite

dramatic. While carrying out some psychic work with a mediumistic young member named Michael Thorburn, David was told that there was a spiritual being next to him. Was he aware of who it was? David tuned in and immediately recognised the being as Pharaoh Akhnaton. Michael confirmed this and said the spirit would now change. David tuned in again and saw a clear picture. Again Michael said this was correct. Then another quite different spirit came through. "And that's when my conscious mind said 'this is a load of hooey!' David remembers: "I saw a soldier around the nineteenth century in a red uniform with two white bands. Then my mind clouded over and my rational mind stopped it all."

At that point David reasoned that either he was reading Michael's mind—which in itself was no mean feat—or the spiritual beings were really there. "Either way, when you have experiences like that you cannot easily forget them," he says. "These images do have a power of their own." In fact, David found the perceptive side of his nature difficult to uncover. He had to work hard, learning to relax and to discover ways of becoming more aware. For him it was easier to be a positive—the handler rather than receiver of energies—and more suitable for his interest in the mental and occult healing work of the Atlanteans.

In the late 1960s, London was changing dramatically: the vibrations were heavier, the atmosphere confusing. The Atlanteans wanted to operate in a purer, more rarefied atmosphere. In other words, they wanted to move to the country. Very seldom did H-A tell the group "you must do this", or "it has to be like that." Although they had a strong impression he wanted them to move away from London, it was up to the group to pick the exact spot psychically.

They 'knew' it had to be west of London. Cheltenham, they decided, 'felt right'. A flourishing branch of the Atlanteans was already established in Cheltenham, and it was nice to have ready-made friends there. But this was not the only reason. When they researched more closely, they saw that the sun and rising signs in the astrological birth chart of the Cheltenham branch was the mirror opposite to those in the birthchart of the society itself: a chance in a million. It was as though the headquarters was destined to complement the Cheltenham branch and vice versa.

Even at this stage of the society's evolution, an idea was vaguely forming that one day there would be some form of Atlantean community. Their idealistic vision was to purchase a property large enough for many members of the society to come together and work towards self-sufficiency. The question of how they would all earn a living never occurred to them! It was with this in mind that the headquarters moved to Cheltenham, and several of the members followed.

The move took place in several stages. Tony and Ann Neate moved first, in October 1970. To all who decided to sell their houses and move to Cheltenham it was a formidable challenge, not least for Tony. At the age of forty he was leaving a bright career in management at Shell, where he had worked for twenty three years since he left school. It was an enormous leap of faith. In 1972 he bought a health food shop and in 1975 also became a representative for J.I. Rodale, an American health food company. Later, when it became impossible to do the two simultaneously he sold the shop and worked exclusively for Rodale.

Ann had continued to sing after her marriage, touring in opera with *The Intimate Opera Company*, comprising four people, three singers and a pianist, under the directorship of Anthony Hopkins. She also broadcast frequently and was still singing professionally at the age of thirty-six, when her first child Semira was born. When her second child Dominic was four, the year they moved to Cheltenham, she decided to give up singing as her life had become rich and fulfilling in other ways.

When the Furlongs, who planned to move to Cheltenham in two or three years, first came to visit Ann and Tony in February 1971, Diane was pregnant and David was unemployed. David had given up his job in the planning office to set up a pony-trekking holiday centre in Somerset, but at the last minute the other couple involved had pulled out. At the time of the visit David was beginning to establish a sideline in a small way, drawing up workplans for people who wanted to make building applications to the council.

As it happened, Tony asked David and Diane if they would pick up a spare key from an estate agent. While they were there they asked about properties, and "just for fun" asked to view the first house on the list. It was a ter-raced cottage that belonged to a builder, and had come on to the market that day. They fell in love with it at once. The price was too good to be true and they made an offer. In eight weeks, in April 1971, they also had moved.

It was only once they had moved to Cheltenham that David and Diane finally became an integral part of The Atlanteans. In the previous year or two, although David had joined in the esoteric side of the work, they had re-mained on the fringe, gradually learning the workings of the society. Diane, however, had been working on her sensitivity in her own way, guided by the understanding that David had received. In fact Diane was to become extremely mediumistic, the negative to David's positive in their partnership, and eventually she, too, was to tune into H-A.

In the meantime, Tricia and Henley Thomas, along with another early Atlantean member, Betty Wood, took over the running of the Ealing branch of the society. Tricia was now leading meditation groups and practising healing. She was also teaching and helping others to develop in the same way. Her own growth of sensitivity, she says, was not a blinding flash, but more like peeling off the layers of an onion. "One more or less slid into it; perhaps going

David and Diane Furlong

over ground of previous lives." In her training Tricia was drawn towards the positive side of occult healing, in contrast to Henley who was already an established sensitive. Over the years, however, Tricia has gradually developed her receptive side, while Henley has started to work on the positive polarity.

Tricia had given up her acting career to start a family, three years after she and Henley were married. They have two children, Deri and Katie. In 1967, Henley also gave up acting to train as a drama teacher. He was working in a London comprehensive, but by the time the society was thinking of moving to Cheltenham he had become disillusioned with state education in general and with comprehensives in particular. With Tony and Ann, Jackie, and also David and Diane, already in Cheltenham, the Thomases decided they would follow in a year or so. They travelled down to Cheltenham from time to time, tentatively house-hunting. Eventually, in July 1972, they sold their flat in Ealing, found a house next-door-but-one to the Furlongs and trusted that a teaching job for Henley would turn up. It did. Tony had seen an advertisement in a local paper for a drama teacher, Henley applied and was offered the post.

One or two other members of the society also moved to Cheltenham. They all met regularly to form a healing and teaching group in a private house of a member of the local branch. But one of the most urgent tasks, H-A told them, was to find a new headquarters. David took responsibility for finding a suitable building, and at the end of 1971, through generous donations and loans from members, they were able to purchase Isis House, at 42 St George's Street. This comprised a meeting room, an office, a reception room, a kitchen, a library and a well-kept garden. The flat overhead earned them valuable working capital. At last the society had firm roots.

By 1971 they felt that the symbol of Uranus had outgrown its purpose. Its positive, dynamic, disruptive

energy had been necessary to get the society off the
ground, and to carry them forward. It created the explo-
sion which brought the Atlanteans into being. H-A had
told them there had been strong opposition to the birth of
the group, not because at that stage it constituted a powerful force for light, but because it stood for an age-old
philosophy that was to be not so much revived as up-
dated. It represented the turning of a full circle. This turning was necessary, he said, not only for the Atlanteans,
but for many other groups, for the state of evolution of the
planet at this moment in time has reached grave propor-
tions. The planet is about to take one of its biggest initiations in which lives will be sacrificed, but from which will
emerge the new man of the future golden age. Mankind
will be given yet another opportunity to right itself.

H-A suggested they consider new ideas for a new symbol. They deliberated for several weeks, but nothing
transpired and finally they turned back to H-A for inspiration. He gave them the symbol of the ankh within the
blazing sun. The ankh: the feminine, receptive principle
symbolised the seed of love, compassion and wisdom.
The sun: the masculine, positive, giving-out principle,
represented the light and warmth through which the seed
grows. Together they manifested the Father/Mother
aspects of the Godhead, creating balance between the
positive and negative polarities. Neither side can be
ignored because each impulse is equally important. True
balance is a perfect fusion between the two, and this
criterion, as explained in the previous chapter, can be
applied to every level of frequency or vibration within the
universe. In fact it is the imbalance of the positive and
negative vibrations relating to the planet which contributes to so much of its trouble.

Let us take the Christian religion. Of all the influences
which have been brought to bear on the Earth, that of
Christianity was the most significant, inasmuch as it was

a very strong effort on the part of the forces of light to
bring the planet back on course. Much of the failure of
the Christian religion to bring peace and tolerance to the
planet is directly due to its failure to maintain a balance
between the polarity of Father/Mother within the
oneness of the Godhead and to present these two
aspects to man. This is lamentable, for in the original
teaching of Jesus Christ the over-emphasis on the
masculine aspect was very much less evident than in the
post-Nicean period.

Two thousand years ago, when the Solar Logos or
Christ spirit took on a body in Palestine, another spirit
representing the negative or polarising aspect should
have incarnated at a different place in the world, but due
to forces of opposition this plan was thwarted and Jesus
was denied a living polarity. Here, indeed, was a spoke
in the wheel of the divine plan. However, the feminine
side, which was known as the Sophia to the early Christians, overshadowed him at the time of his baptism by
John, after which he was able to proceed with his occult
work and pursue the purpose of his incarnation.

Descriptions of the Sophia or wisdom can be found
throughout the literature of the early Christians, and
were an accepted part of early Christian teachings. The
Gnostics had a gospel which they called the Pistis
Sophia or faith/wisdom but as this, like many other
early Christian documents, was seen to be incompatible
with Pauline teachings, it was ignored by the main body
of the Church as time went by.

Looking back to the early religions you will find that
there is a Father, a Mother and a Son or Daughter concept, that is a trinity. You have the positive and negative
uniting to produce a third force; the manifest. This
became changed in Christianity. The Mother concept
was dropped or relegated and into its place fluttered a
nebulous transcendent force known as the Holy Spirit.
And so the all-powerful father, his beloved son and

another undefined spirit became the Trinity, and tilted the whole concept of the Godhead into an ultra-positive masculine direction.

The result of this was an imbalance which over-activated the aggressive male principle in younger souls, causing belligerence and intolerance. Consider the number of wars that have been fought in the name of Christianity. Look at the number of people who have been tortured physically and mentally in the name of a founder to whom such rites would have been abhor-rent. Looking at the structure of the Christian religion today—not the individuals who belong to it, but the institution as a concept—one wonders how the true teachings of Christ ever manage to come through.

Over the past two thousand years Christianity has carried itself forward with a tremendous impulse under the mistaken impression that it was the only interpreta-tion of the Godhead that was right. Unfortunately, its success in the form which it chose to adopt has not helped to maintain a balance on this planet. Although the feminine aspect of the Godhead is well-represented in the eastern religions, somehow the twain never managed to come together and exchange ideas.

According to H-A the critical situation we find ourselves in on Earth has occurred for many interrelated reasons. Cen-tral to his teaching however is that at this present time, the planet Earth is not being influenced by its rightful deva, but by intelligences that do not follow the paths of light. A planetary deva is a spirit of advanced evolution from the elemental kingdoms that guides a planet in the same way that a guardian angel helps an individual.

Every sphere of evolution on a planet has free will as to how much it accepts or rejects the deva's guidance. On the other hand, the guidance from a deva is power-ful and undoubtedly will affect the overall character of the planet. Every planet in the solar system has a deva, each of which is at a different stage of evolution. It influences the planet according to its own stage of wisdom, affecting not only its own sphere of rulership, but also other planets in the solar system. The deva may use the planet for its own evolution and a wise deva will allow itself to progress with the planet. But this is not always so.

It is possible for a planetary deva to misguide the planet within its care. No spirit is perfect until it reaches the Ultimate or Godhead and it may slip backwards. The present devic influence on Earth is not all it should be. Twice in the history of man there have been cosmic disturbances caused by an upset in the magnetic balance within the solar system. First when a large part of the continent of Mu or Lemuria sank beneath the Pacific Ocean, and secondly when the continent of Atlantis sank around 7,000 BC at the end of the solar age of Cancer.

The second cataclysm, caused by a tilt in the planet's axis, occurred when the imbalance of the Earth and the corruption of man during the latter days of Atlantis caused a wave of negative energy from another part of the universe to be drawn to this planet, which has since had a degenerate influence on the minds of men.

This 'fall', as it has been described, is recognised in every belief system, each with its own name for the offending 'fallen one': the Greeks called him Typhon, the ancient Egyptians, Set, and the Christians have equated Satan with the deva Lucifer. Like attracts like, and Lucifer, says H-A, found Earth ready to receive its malign influence and the rightful deva of Earth, the Archangel Michael, was deposed.

The blame for this stage of imbalance, explains H-A, cannot be wholly attributed to wrongful devic influence, because the power of the rightful governor of Earth could never have been usurped had the actions and reactions of those evolving on Earth been different. The amount of influence or power any deva has over a planet is a reflection of the life and thoughts of those living on that world.

The battle on that grand devic scale is reflected within each of us. In our own thinking we are feeding either the forces of light symbolised by Michael, or the forces of darkness, symbolised by Lucifer. It is through our own minds that the battle is ensuing. If for some reason mankind was suddenly to pull itself together, dispense with all ideas of war and suffering and fearlessly set out to bring understanding and love to Earth, then Lucifer could no longer maintain its influence over us. It can only retain its control by our own volition.

Unfortunately this malign influence on Earth has encouraged man to feel insecure and inferior; it has ensured that he does not see himself as he really is. This has taught man to snatch greedily at those aspects of life which make for his comfort and give him power. So one could say that some of the early councils of the Christian Church provided some of the greatest triumphs for the Luciferian influence which now seems to have such a close grip on man.

As this influence gradually gained in power, through man's own ego it encouraged the emotions of fear and insecurity. It imbued the subconscious minds of those early men of the Church with the thought that security lay only in the supremacy of the Christian religion and in those privileged to gain favour through its auspices. To achieve this form of intolerance and arrogance it was necessary to emphasise the masculine or positive aspect of the Ultimate and so God became to many men a force which demanded of them that they practise belligerence, inflict suffering and torture and seek power in His name. The desire to destroy, to hurt one's fellow beings and be hurt in return became a way of religious belief. All this could have been avoided if only a balance had been kept and the feminine/receptive aspect of the Godhead, the Sophia had not been lost.

It was now essential that the Atlanteans play their part in trying to correct this imbalance, to restore the missing polarity. It was time for the re-emergence of the feminine. Choosing a name from the pages of mythology, which the wise ones of the past revered as the mother of all, the Isis concept of the Atlanteans was born.

There are other names which might have been chosen: Mary, Keridwen, Demeter, Tanith, Dana, all names which past civilisations have bestowed on the divine Mother, and which are still meaningful, more meaningful than some of the later symbols. The names themselves are but symbols; it is the understanding they present that is significant. Isis and Osiris are not people, or entities, or even levels of power, but levels of consciousness, symbols of archetypal influences and inclinations and ways in which power is used, which have to be handled with delicacy and sensitivity. For the higher you reach towards the light, the lower you can be pulled down by the powers of darkness. The balance is a delicate one.

The new symbol reawakened an interest in the Egyptian pantheon of archetypes, the psychological principles which govern life within each human being. (Diane, in particular, still finds this mythology a useful tool in her work.) In the early days of the society, amongst the group of spirit guides that came through to them, Akhnaton was especially strong. Tony always knew when Akhnaton was around because he projected a 'social' atmosphere. Akhnaton made him want to laugh! The spirit was not on such a fine wavelength as H-A, but seemed nearer to themselves in vibration. He appeared to act as H-A's 'right-hand man', and Tony would occasionally tune into H-A through Akhnaton, as a way of 'stepping down' the energies.

The wings of Isis were necessary in order to bring forth in people's consciousness the feminine aspect of the Godhead. Isis was frequently depicted with her arms, like wings, outstretched to protect all creatures, with the wings being symbolic also of soaring to spiritual heights. The Isis concept in the Atlanteans did not replace all that had been said before, but complemented it and set yet another challenge.

> For the feminine principle must be correctly handled so that it, in turn, does not become over-exaggerated or the imbalance will fall in the opposite direction. People would tend to be indolent, negative and without a forward impetus. This is what happened in Atlantis, which was in fact the archetype of the Isis vibration, and this ultimately caused its downfall, for exactly the opposite reasons to those that are causing the downfall of the present civilisation. Isis must also have her Osiris. This is the way to bring about a new Atlantis. It is a challenge which, if risen to in the right way, will help to make a positive and determined attempt to bring light to dispel the clouds of doom.

The new inspiration brought an added warmth and feminine receptivity to the society. The symbol brought through strongly a new and important aspect of the work. It represented a transformation and a perceptible move towards the spiritual.

Chapter Five

In Transition

It was an exciting time in the history of the Atlanteans. The new symbol, the ankh contained within the sun, signalled the beginning of a new impetus. Helio-Arcanophus came through to them a little less often than he had at the beginning; he preferred that they translate his words into actions in their own way. The headquarters of the society became a focal point for members and a source of inspiration for many. They held social events as well as public lectures and tried to involve the members' children in a positive way, holding special festivals and occasional dramatic presentations. They made puppets of Egyptian gods, for example, and the children spoke the voices of characters in the story of Isis and Osiris. Tricia remembers one particular Pageant of the Elements, performed by the children in the garden of Tony and Ann's Elizabethan cottage. The child playing 'water' had a fish-tail made around her lower half which totally immobilised her. She had to be pushed around in a suitably decorated wheelbarrow.

H-A had always instilled in the Atlanteans a sympathy and respect for all life. His philosophy teaches that evolution is like a tree with many branches. The spirit of man is in no way superior to the spirit of an animal or a spirit of the plant or mineral kingdoms. The brain of man may be more advanced, but not necessarily his spirit.

Within the Universe exist an infinite number of forms of evolution, each having its place in the scheme of things. A human being is but one of these. A spirit progresses along its chosen path and evolves until it eventually reaches a stage where it has gained complete understanding and harmony with all other forms of life. In order to do so, it is not necessary for that spirit to undergo every form of experience. When it rejoins the Godhead, although it will share in the all-wise state existing there, it will not have exactly the same approach as its neighbours: it will contribute a unique record of experience, adding to what is already there, and thus it will retain its individuality. Hence the Godhead in its infinity is itself expanding.

When a new thought or spirit first leaves the Godhead, it has the gift of free will to experience in whichever way it wishes. Some spirits choose human existence, others decide to enter the animal, vegetable or mineral kingdoms. There are streams of evolution that do not require a physical body at all, yet which affect your everyday life even though you may be unaware of them.

Very few people give much thought to what may appear to be mere processes of nature; the vast majority of men and women neither see nor hear the beings or intelligences that express themselves by serving the planet at this level. These beings known as the spirits of fire, air, earth and water are collectively known as 'the spirits of the elements' and individually as 'elementals'. The term 'elemental' does not refer to any astral shell, poltergeist, earthbound spirit, thought-form or elementary (less-evolved) entity. These elementals originate from the Godhead in exactly the same way as human beings, but at an early stage they choose a different form of expression. Although the spirits of the elements assist the planet as a whole, they are rather more concerned with the structure of the sphere itself than the life forms on it.

The names given to these beings by the ancients were: 'salamanders' for spirits of fire, 'sylphs' for spirits of the air, 'ondines' or 'nymphs' for water spirits and 'gnomes' for earth spirits. Some people, either by training themselves in the art of perception or by means of a natural gift, are able to see these beings and observe the part they play. The beauty and innocence of children often attract them to 'come forth from their own kind' and to make friends. The child who claims to have seen some 'little people' may be speaking the truth.

Earth elementals are often seen as gnomes of varying sizes and appearances, while air elementals sometimes appear as fairies with wings. It must be understood, however, that it is man who has created these images of his elemental cousins, not the elementals themselves; they merely adopt a guise by which they will be recognisable to human beings. A child would not connect a gnome with a lump of quartz or a sylph with a beam of light. These forms that they adopt for recognition will probably change as man's concept of them changes.

Elemental spirits do not evolve in the same manner as mankind. They begin their evolutionary journey as a single element or as part of the group soul of a particular element, and as they advance they become more and more individualised. Normally the group soul of an element stays intact and does not individualise unless for some special purpose or job. When an element has learnt all that it can of its own element, it begins to seek experience in one of the other three. These it will master one at a time; so, although many elementals are of a single nature, others have a twofold or threefold nature. Once an elemental masters all four elements it is said to have won its fourfold nature, whereupon it ascends to the planes of the devas and will assist in the guidance of planets. Human spirits are also fourfold by nature, but these four aspects are not as individually accentuated as they are in a fourfold elemental or deva.

Elementals are not androgynous and the nearest to a true description is to say that some of them would be regarded as psychically positive and others psychically negative. In this way they endeavour to harmonise with their opposite polarity among human beings. Thus a person who is psychically on a negative vibration would be more in sympathy with a positive elemental, whereas a man or woman on a positive psychic vibration would attract a negative elemental, since they would in each case be complementary to each other.

Fire and air are represented as being positive and water and earth as negative, but this in no way determines the individual polarity of any one particular elemental, any more than the polarity of a planet makes all its inhabitants of one kind. Each elemental is an individual in its own right and, should it wish to be seen, will appear in a female guise if it is on a negative vibration, and in a male form if it is on a positive one.

Different types of people have various tastes, aptitudes and affinities. Some are attracted to water, for example, while others dislike it. There are those who love the bite of a keen wind or the heat of the sun on a summer's day. There are those who love mountains, while others feel instinctively hemmed in and oppressed by them. Many people dislike extremes of heat or cold, and there are people who carry their aversion to the air elementals so far that the slightest draught is a source of annoyance to them. Although each person will always have an affinity with one of the four elements in particular, an overall sympathy is desirable, and that strange instinctive dread of the elements which haunts the minds of so many people would be dispelled by an understanding of all four of them and a recognition of them in their own psyche.

All forms of elemental life are experiencing and evolving just as human beings are. While an elemental will
undergo an entirely different set of experiences, it will
gain an increasing understanding of the life undergone
by humans, just as they will, in time, begin to comprehend the existence and purpose of the elementals. On
the higher planes, all forms tend gradually to overlap,
and the guidance of planets is not only undertaken by
devas, advanced spirits of the elemental kingdoms, but
by exalted human spirits that have reached a similar
stage of evolution.

The emergence of mankind on Earth has rather
eclipsed the vital contribution that these spirits of fire,
air, earth and water have always made to the life of the
planet. When Earth was first born of gaseous mass, it
was the elementals whose life-force formed the various
chemicals and moulded the structure of the globe.
These beings are not perfect and are learning just as you
are. They also make mistakes, hence the physical evolution of the world has not always been as smooth as
might be desired. But they are still very actively
concerned with the planet. Owing to the inevitable
interplay between humanity and these beings, the two
forms of evolution are very much in sympathy with one
another. This is why nature rebels when an excess of
evil or unbalanced thought is projected by man.

When man has learned to understand and co-operate
with his elemental cousins, many natural hazards will
be prevented. The animal kingdom, which is in closer
touch with these spirits, exemplifies this: notice how
animals will sense a coming earthquake and evacuate an
area long before it occurs. Even man's most sophisti-
cated equipment can only record a tremor, it cannot
anticipate it. The influence of the elementals on Earth
has been somewhat undermined by the misguidance
the planet has been suffering. When the rightful deva
returns to govern Earth, the elemental influences will be

felt much more strongly and this will greatly benefit mankind as a whole.

Although, like humans, these beings are composed of thought, they operate on a 'sharper' frequency than mankind and one that is radioactive by nature. According to H-A, elementals can communicate with man and achieve the best results by telepathically transmitting thought pictures into the mind of a sensitive person, which he or she can in turn translate into words. Spirits of the elements can help psychically in many ways to broaden man's understanding. For example, a gnome can present a mental picture of the geological structure of the planet, thus helping on a scientific level. A salamander can give invaluable assistance to a person studying physics and electricity.

> The secret of working with elementals is to seek their help in accordance with the nature of their own element, and not expect a single element to do all and sundry when in fact it is limited to working within its own element. The student learns to raise his vibration in order to be able to communicate with the elemental and deva kingdoms. Very few actually succeed in raising themselves sufficiently to contact a planetary deva. It is far easier to contact the spirits of the elements, who will willingly help the student provided he is on the right path and working along the lines of cosmic law.

It would pay handsome dividends, says H-A, to develop this affinity with the spirits of the elements and work in co-operation with them, in order to learn more about the planet and how to cope with it in a natural way. The Atlanteans work consciously with elemental spirits during their planetary healing work. It sounds grandiose, says David, but these forces are open to anyone whose mind is open to receiving their vibrations. If, for example, they are trying to heal man's consciousness in relation to the destruction of trees in South America, they will ask the relevant spirits to help them in their work by adding thoughts to their own. All spiritual beings need this link with man's consciousness to filter down certain spiritual forces.

David remembers during one particular study group, he asked an elemental spirit working with them to present itself. The spirit sat on a woman's hand and she described what she was experiencing. She said she felt a beautiful crystalline structure with many facets. Then it slowly started to change and become more fluid. Finally it was like a mist. In fact, says David, she was describing the water elemental going through all its stages of experience: ice, water and steam. "She had sensed and described it exactly, and then said she didn't know what it was!"

Within a year of introducing the concept of Isis the Mother, representing a renewed link with nature and the elements, the Atlanteans began to celebrate the four Festivals of Isis, held regularly at the summer and winter solstices and the spring and autumn equinoxes. Each festival includes a simple ceremony which lasts an hour or so and is essentially a meditation on that particular season and its respective elements. The aim is to attune to the rhythm of the planet and of the natural world.

The spring festival, The Festival of Flowers, celebrates the element of air and the time of year when the life-giving forces of nature are awakening from their winter sleep; a time of rebirth, a budding and flowering of those energies that have been stirring within us during the winter months. Flowers are associated with fairies or air elementals and during the festival gifts of some form of plant life are exchanged.

The Atlanteans adopted the element of water and the symbol of the ship for the summer festival, even though it might have seemed more natural to choose the fire element, since the sun is at its highest at that time. Their inspiration was to fill the ship with thoughts of love and light and launch it to travel around the world, taking with it that love and light. Every summer someone would build a model boat which, during the festival, they would take to a nearby stretch of water. One summer they took their boat, with its symbolic sail, to a point on the River Severn and launched it with due ceremony. The boat had just reached approximately four hundred yards downstream and was about to go round a bend in the river, when a small motor launch came up in the other direction. The occupants saw their boat, thought it had escaped and brought it back! "We had to thank them politely and then wait until they had gone further upstream to launch it again!" remembers Ann, laughing at the memory.

On another occasion they took their 'ship' to the South Wales coast. The wind that day was very strong and the sea quite choppy. Standing on the shore in their wellington boots and macs they tried to launch the boat, but the waves kept bringing it back. It was a long time before anyone could wade out far enough to set it on its way, just as three coast guards came past in their yellow sou'westers, totally bemused at the sight of thirty or forty people trying to propel a tiny boat out to sea. After a year or two they decided to launch their ship more symbolically!

Autumn celebrates the element of fire in the Festival of Stars and Light. Candles were dedicated to the beings beyond the planet and beyond the solar system, whatever their nature. In the early days each member in turn would light a candle from the one in front, but that, too, had its problems. To avoid the mess from dropped candle grease, after a year or two they decided to light a circle of just twelve candles with one in the middle. Today, the person conducting the ceremony lights the first one and then invites anyone else to dedicate the remaining ones in whatever way they wish. In winter, the Festival of Music and Arts, affirming the element of inner growth and rebirth, links closely with the festival of Christmas.

The four festivals are the only activity of the Atlanteans that could be considered ritualistic, although they have certainly always used symbols mentally for healing and protection to focus the power of thought. In fact, one amusing story relates how in the early days a clairvoyant who came into a healing meeting declared that the atmosphere was extraordinary. She constantly saw crosses over people's heads as each healer thought strongly of the cross—the symbol of balance between Earth and spirit—in the process of his healing work. But H-A stressed to them that ritual is simply a psychological framework for thought and that today, in the mental age of Aquarius, it is no longer necessary to man's spiritual enlightenment.

All of you are using some form of ritual in your spiritual seeking, but each one of you uses it in a different way and some of you need more ritual than others. It is not wrong, but the spirit eventually reaches a stage of understanding in which ritual becomes an unnecessary prop. Yet to suggest that it is unnecessary is tantamount to saying that if you are going to build a mining shaft and your geometry is perfect you will not need to prop it up. You do not possess the tools, nor do you have the skill to achieve this. The type of prop used in a mining shaft is one which is designed to withstand the pressure of the earth around it and which requires the minimum of effort to establish.

In spiritual seeking it is up to you as to how many props you use, but the more you use the more you are limiting yourself to them. You have only to walk into a church and kneel down and you have performed a ritual, you have adopted a physical attitude which helps you to pray. When you repeat a set of prayers you are performing a ritual; using a symbol is performing a ritual. Certain rituals do carry powers which vary in efficacy according to their age, their use and the psychic power of their originators; but the power is limited to the ritual. Whereas, pure thought, if used correctly, has no limitations. All rituals are limited to the amount of thought with which they have become associated over the years.

When you begin to allow your thought to expand to the higher levels of consciousness, the more you can unfetter the mind and body from limitation, the more you are likely to find a new understanding which will enable you to raise yourself above the practical, material abyss in which you find yourself on this planet today.

As you go forward in your seeking, of course, you are going to use a certain amount of ritual with which to discipline yourself. If you do not you will find it very difficult to live in the tension-making conditions of modern living. But it is important to use ritual without becoming too dependent on it. This applies to ritual in any shape or form. Many people find great solace and devotional expression through simple rituals and there are those people who are able to use symbology as a means of understanding and communicating with the spirit world. If this is the case then you should try to avoid the trap of over-complication. For example, where the symbol representing the Father/Mother God is used, as it is in the Atlantean symbol, it is the Godhead behind the symbol that you seek, not the symbol itself. Ultimately the mind is more powerful than the enacted ritual and by the close of the Aquarian age man will have learned to use his mind sufficiently to enable him to dispense with the ritualistic prop altogether.

Inevitably the shifts in vibration, heralded by the new symbol, brought fundamental changes in the society and precipitated alterations in its membership. Some members veered away, while others were drawn. And when the vicar of a local parish informed the group that healing should be practised only under the auspices of the Church, this too created a strong and sudden rift with two or three core members. This worried some of those remaining, but H-A made it clear that every society must change and should not be afraid of movement: each individual has to seek the spiritual home that suits him best. It was this philosophical approach that helped them to accept that such changes were best for all concerned.

The Atlanteans existed because a group of friends doing psychic exploration had, almost by accident, found themselves tuning into a philosophy of a high order. In the 1950s the people involved had been young and unsophisticated and H-A had taught them the principles of the universe and psychic energies in a fairly dramatic way. If he had come through to them in a more gentle way, being the kind of people they were, they possibly would not have responded. As H-A says, his teachings can be read and understood on many levels. No matter what a teaching represents, it is those who receive it who have invoked it and mould and interpret it. In those early days, people were interested in phenomena. As well as an appreciation of the philosophy, the Atlanteans were particularly interested in psychic development and so for many years there was a strong emphasis on this aspect.

Their long-term study of universal energies had stood them in good stead, but by the 1970s the society was beginning to shift in emphasis, becoming by intention more of a teaching and less of a psychic group. There were fewer public trances, but a team of speakers was slowly developing who were able to expound the philosophy. Gradually the enormity of the content of H-A's teachings had begun to penetrate. They could concentrate on a more serious commitment to the healing work in conjunction with the deeper implications of the Atlantean philosophy. This move, however, did cause a further fragmentation of the society.

Up to this point Jackie had been the pivot upon which the Atlanteans had revolved: her leadership as an occultist and psychic researcher was unparalleled. But within herself she felt restless and unfulfilled. In 1975, Jackie's personal life suddenly took her right away from headquarters, allowing her to develop her talent in a different direction which suited her better. Since that time she has followed the more deeply occult and academic side of the work—she is now an author, journalist and broadcaster, writing under the name Murry Hope—but H-A is still her teacher and spiritual guide. A distinctive attribute of H-A is that he has never made himself exclusive to anyone. He continues to give teachings through several channels and is picked up by many outside the inner structure of the Atlanteans, possibly even known to other groups under a different title. What emerges in each case is a philosophical expression coloured by the people concerned, according to their overall experience.

Inevitably, Jackie's departure plunged the society into a precarious period of adjustment. Other members left with her, which caused a certain amount of disarray. Around that time, Tony found that the public lectures were creating too much strain. Even in the heyday, when H-A came through four or five times a week, if he attempted to do more he 'went to pieces'. He points out that sensitives frequently break down or are subject to illness through overstrain.

Several years before, H-A had mooted the idea that the Atlanteans should begin to run courses. So far they had not felt particularly motivated to do so. In 1976, however, they established a yearly programme of two residential weekend courses, held at educational centres like Hawkwood College, an adult education centre near Stroud, run under the auspices of the Anthroposophical Society. The courses covered such topics as the art of self-healing or complementary therapies, such as homeopathy and acupuncture, with lectures and some practical work. They felt this was an ideal way of reaching the general

Where there's love

public who were becoming interested in complementary medicine, as indeed they themselves had become in the last few years.

This was the era of the annual Festival of Mind, Body and (later) Spirit, held at Olympia in London. To a certain degree the society was now 'going public', joining the regular New Age scene. Introverted in the past, they felt they were ready to move outwards and to link up with like-minded souls. In fact, the Atlanteans was a prime mover in bringing spiritual groups together, something which in those days was virtually unheard of.

As the membership reshuffled, the three families—the Neates, the Furlongs and the Thomases—were drawing closer together, and Diane, who had had two children, Claire and Maaten, became more firmly part of the core group. Cheltenham had always been regarded as a temporary move before the society set up a wider community, and now they were again discussing the possibility of finding a property where they could all live together. The members enthusiastically made regular exploratory expeditions around the Cotswolds, but ultimately it was only the three families who felt they were prepared to commit themselves.

The six discussed deeply what sort of place might be suitable, how it could work and how they would iron out all the personal difficulties that were bound to arise. In the end, however, although they viewed a few properties, they admitted that perhaps this was not quite the right time. Tony was committed as a councillor to the Cheltenham Borough Council and Henley, who had finally given up teaching at the local comprehensive, was now committed to teaching for several years at Wynstones, the Rudolf Steiner school in Gloucester.

When the Atlanteans moved to Cheltenham, first the Neates and then the Thomases sent their children to Wynstones. During the Thomases' first term a letter was sent to parents, informing them that two teachers were about to leave. Were there any teacher-parents who might be interested in filling these posts? To be accepted as a teacher at a Steiner school depends more on the quality of the person than on previous training in the education. As a parent, sympathetic to the Steiner ideals, and already a trained teacher, Henley was asked to join the staff.

Teaching at Wynstones, Henley was steeped in a ready-made spiritual movement—Anthroposophy—which encompassed many areas including education, science and medicine. He certainly felt able to "throw in my lot" where his professional life was concerned. In 1974, Tricia also joined the teaching staff, as a part-time handwork teacher. She was soon involved in doing drama with the children and she and Henley often performed at fund-raising events. For Tricia it was a joy being associated with the Steiner movement in education. It complemented her belief that children should be educated in a spiritual way, and for her it was the spiritual impulse working in a practical way.

Nonetheless, both Henley and Tricia knew that their true spiritual commitment was to H-A and the work of the Atlanteans. In general, Steiner's approach through 'the science of man' and the philosophy of the Atlanteans went hand in hand. Henley and Tricia looked for the similarities, not the differences, and the school for its part accepted them both with love and understanding. They found this period in their lives a challenging and fulfilling experience. Ann and Tony decided to stay put in Cheltenham. David and Diane however, were still keen to live in a community. David was building up his surveying and planning work, and when in 1976 he saw the potential of buying an old house in Gloucestershire, the Furlongs joined forces with their next door neighbours in Cheltenham, Judy and Mick Jewell, to set up a more communal enterprise. The two couples moved into Highfield House in August 1976, divided it into two separate living units, and for five years ran it as a centre and guest house,

Henley and Tricia Thomas

offering regular courses and workshops in meditation and healing.

Their time at Highfield House proved an invaluable experience; they learned an enormous amount. The Furlongs' psychic and spiritual abilities improved in leaps and bounds, and Diane, who had always felt the youngest and least experienced member of the Atlanteans, was now doing trance or inspirational work, using the Egyptian symbols which had opened up so much of her psyche. At last she felt she could hold her own alongside the other members of the Atlanteans. Above all, Highfield House turned out to be a pioneering project for what would eventually be a much broader and more deeply committed notion of community living: Runnings Park.

Chapter Six

A Family of Atlanteans

Helio-Arcanophus understood. The three families had, for the time being, gone their separate ways. Tricia and Henley had moved to Stroud and were involved at Wynstones; David and Diane were at Highfield House. Tony was working hard at the health food business and Ann, who had always been responsible for editing H-A's teachings for the booklets, continued to produce a regular Atlantean newsletter alongside the magazine, which was then edited by other members of the society. H-A accepted that they were not quite ready for more committed community living.

H-A was endlessly patient with their failings and foibles. He made suggestions, and it was up to the group to take them up when they were ready. He never put forward opinions that could not be rejected if they chose. "He never pushes, only suggests, it is a very subtle thing," says David. "Often it is only when you think about it afterwards that you realise he has said something profound. You never feel 'H-A says this, therefore it is right'. Whatever he has presented it has been in the spirit of 'in my opinion', or 'I feel that', or 'do you think you have got this quite right?' I think we sometimes let him down in the sense that he asked us to do things and we didn't do them. But if anyone got anxious, it was us!'

Yet H-A did make it plain that he wanted them to set up

a centre as soon as possible; not so much as a community, but as a spiritual centre of light. He told them firmly that he felt it was important for the state of the world and that as we moved towards the end of the century, the teachings should be made available to a wider audience.

For many centuries clouds of fear and suspicion have penetrated into the hearts of mankind, resulting in a basic feeling of insecurity that expresses itself as greed and an inane desire for power: power over one's fellow beings in an effort to balance out the insecurity. Man in his material achievements has lost all sense of values and the individual has been forced to live more and more on his nerves. This is because man has allowed power to become his god.

Why is it that the whole man becomes out of balance so easily? It is important to maintain a balance between the chakric centres, those connecting points of energy between the various bodies through which the life force flows and which represent different levels of beingness. If energies are expressed only through the lower or denser chakras, that is only through physical and materialistic activity, without the uplifting and balancing quality of spiritual or higher ideals, then one's life force is functioning on a level that is the most vulnerable where the forces of darkness are concerned.

It is sometimes difficult to choose between the direction that one knows inside to be right and that which offers temptation, excitement, stimulation or material gain. Yet true spiritual seeking is the most rewarding path of all, for its borders are not limited as are those of the lower energies. Where the higher energies of love, service and illumination are concerned, there are no limitations at all. The spirit can transcend the physical and subtle bodies and experience the higher realms of the universe.

It is important for each individual to reassess this

knowledge within himself because in the years that lie
ahead mankind is going to face its most supreme
challenge, the challenge that will decide whether the
forces of light are going to infiltrate into every corner of
the planet or whether the forces of darkness will drag
this planet down.

With the evolution of the brain and the physical body
and the expansion of the ego within man, much has
been learned during recent centuries and, in particular,
during this century. Man has regained knowledge concerning nuclear power, the atom and the fundamental
physical structure of all things. He has learned much
about electronics. He is beginning to rediscover certain
ways of using sound and vibration and how all these
things play a part in the universe. He has begun to
understand time in relation to other dimensions. The
acquisition of knowledge needs to be tempered with
wisdom and responsibility and so, during the coming
years, it will require even greater efforts on the part of
all who are working for the forces of light to spread forth
spiritual understanding.

The Atlanteans admit candidly that they have always
displayed an unusual reticence. They have long known
that the teachings should be spread more widely, but
there has never been a powerful 'collective will' in that
direction. True, they produced booklets on H-A's
philosophy and publish a regular magazine for Atlantean
members. But, whereas other groups "leap to attention
and rush to do whatever their spiritual teacher asks", with
the Atlanteans there has always been a certain reluctance.
The fact that H-A asked for a more popular book to be
written ten years ago, is a case in point!

Other societies spend a great deal of time trying to
persuade people to join them. On the contrary, the
Atlanteans have never overtly advertised themselves.
They have always adopted the attitude that if someone is

interested in their way of thinking and understands its use and value, they will unconsciously be drawn. They have actively tried hard not to turn the society into a cult, or to present H-A as a guru figure to be worshipped. Inevitably there were times when members tried to put the leaders on a pedestal, but one of the special characteristics of Atlantean teaching is that it demands independence.

The Atlantean society carries a flavour; an essence that works within those who feel attuned. Unlike other philosophers, H-A has never been keen on enunciating in detail, which he feels can be a trap. We are all individual and unique; we all think differently. While some people do thirst for knowledge on a detailed level, a broad philosophy allows for individuality of approach. Where the future is concerned H-A has always taken the attitude that there is no fixed future or plan for the planet, only that which it is creating for itself. God does not control the evolution of the universe; it is controlled by all the thought which exists through universal infinity, he says. The Godhead is the fountain Source from which springs all thought or spirit; it offers love, mercy and understanding, but does not dictate as to what transpires. If it did it would merely be commanding all thought to follow its own line of experience and, as such all experience would be superfluous and unnecessary. God allows us to make our own experiences and to deviate if we wish.

It requires a certain sense of independence and security to operate without detailed guidance, and an acceptance of one of H-A's deepest principles, that we must all reach a stage of self-responsibility. This tenet of 'self-responsibility' is a spiritual aspect that most religions ignore. To a patriarchal religion such as Christianity, self-responsibility takes away the power to control from the authority at the top.

Nonetheless, the Atlanteans agree that they have perhaps been over-cautious in hiding their light under a bushel, and Tony is the first to admit that, although not

deliberate, this in part is due to his own reluctance and
fears. His lurking sense of guilt, his paradoxical feeling
about being the main sensitive of the Atlanteans, was a
stumbling block. Once he left Shell, his paranoia about
being the medium for a philosophical teaching, no longer
mattered. He was quite happy to talk openly about H-A
and his experiences as a sensitive. Yet, while on the one
hand he accepted deep down that he had chosen this
path, and that part of his karma in this life was to channel
these teachings, on the other hand, a fraction of him still
remained sceptical and rejected that role.

Vindication for the society's unwillingness to go public
more wholeheartedly was that in spite of the members'
deep commitment to H-A and his teachings, it had never
totally dominated their lives. Other groups set themselves
up as a business or charitable foundation, from which
participants drew their incomes. The Atlanteans all had
income-earning jobs to do. In that sense the Atlanteans
was a part-time, almost spare-time, activity and depended
on how much time could be allocated to it.

But there was no doubt that H-A was telling them more
and more forcefully that he wanted them ultimately
to accept a greater responsibility for disseminating his
teachings and, further, to work at understanding some of
the inner spiritual levels more fully. Within two and a half
years of the Furlongs' move to Highfield House, H-A was
urging the three couples to look seriously for somewhere
else to live, and to come together as a group to help spread
this new perception. He implied that in a sense their own
individual lives were unimportant in the light of this particular task, and that they had chosen before incarnation
to undertake this work. It was their particular karma in
this life.

> Karma is the universal law of cause and effect. That is
> to say, every action has a reaction, or, in human terms,
> 'As a man sows, so shall he reap'. In other words, what

you did in the past is affecting you now, and what you are doing now is shaping your future.

Once free from a body, a discarnate spirit looks back over its record to date and, as a result, determines the sort of earthly existence it next wishes to undergo. Some of this future karma will be determined by the spirit's most recent lifetime on Earth, but if a wise choice is made it will also be a complement to its overall evolution.

For instance, a particular spirit might decide to undergo an experience as a sailor who will be drowned at sea. It will be helped and guided by higher spirits to choose a suitable body that will provide the requisite experience. Because this spirit is not bound by time and space, it can scan its coming Earth life and see the path it will take. It will not see the details of that life, but the milestones, the important events. It sees, say, that in this coming life it will run away from home and go to sea; that it will not marry but will meet up with a close friend from a previous life and see the world; that it owes this friend a debt of gratitude and wishes to repay it in some way. Having thus ascertained the overall plan or karma of this coming incarnation, it would enter that body at the time of conception.

But in this case and in every other case, it is up to your individual free will whether or not you fulfil the karma of each incarnation. Selecting this or that life does not amount to predestination once you are incarnate. Your free will ensures that you can alter course whenever you wish. Fate in its truest sense is not what lies ahead of you, it is the outcome of how *you* handle your life.

No two spirits have ever trodden an identical path of evolution; each chooses its own individual itinerary. This free choice is made by the spirit outside the body, before incarnation, because once it has been reborn as a person here on Earth, that person is subject to prevailing laws, environment, world conditions, and the many other factors that impose restrictions on the expression of free will. This is the challenge the spirit takes on when it incarnates—to express itself within the confines of physical life. You chose your physical body before you entered this life. Having incarnated, you are still free to choose the finer details of your experience, to make the best or worst of your life, to fulfil it or to let it drift aimlessly—or even to embark on a career of cruelty and destruction. And you are making that choice every day.

A spirit *could* complete its entire evolutionary karma in one lifetime, although this would be very exceptional; it usually does so during a number of lives—tens, hundreds or even thousands. Some spirits incarnate many times and others very few. There is no fixed number of incarnations as it is up to the individual concerned. Similarily, you will meet the person who has returned to settle what is sometimes called a karmic debt incurred by wrong-doing in a previous incarnation. He can work off this karmic debt in the first five years of his life, or in one crucial moment, or it may take him a lifetime—and even more, in which case his spirit will have to return to 'balance the books' in yet another Earth life.

Of one thing the six were certain; theirs was indeed a karmic relationship. They had each elected to take this path in life and because of previous lives together including one or more on the continent of Atlantis, had a karma to fulfil.

At the height of its glory, Atlantis which lasted some ten thousand years, was a garden of Eden if ever there was one, an almost perfect state of existence for humankind. These men and women, who were in many respects more advanced than the people of today, knew many secrets of science and the universe which have since been lost—secrets which will not be restored to man until he has learned to show the Earth and his fellows the proper respect.

The inhabitants of this young island continent recognised a supreme force which they believed was responsible for and ruled over their own land and all other lands, seas and skies. To our Atlantean forebears this force was a Father/Mother God and its physical manifestation was the great star—Sun. Only the priesthood could communicate with the spirit forms emanating from this divine source, but physically the Sun was there for all.

The high priest of early Atlantis was the ruler of the state as well as of temple matters. He bore the title of High Priest of the Sun, which was handed down from earliest times. These rulers were chosen by the elders according to their spiritual status, ascertained by etheric sight. Thus no one ever attained such a rank without the wisdom to shoulder the responsibilities it entailed. Below the chief High Priest was a priestly hierarchy. Candidates for the priesthood were chosen at a very early age, under spiritual guidance and in accordance with their own inner status. The senior priests could tell at once whether a child would be suitable for training as, say, a sensitive or healer. The priests were also the scientists, astronomers, mathematicians, doctors and administrators, according to their individual ability and aptitude.

The continent lay in the southern hemisphere, as did the country now known as England—such was the angle of the Earth's axis in those days. As we see the globe today, the northern part of the Atlantean land mass would lie approximately between the British Isles and Canada—much further north than is usually supposed—and Ireland would face directly west to the old capital city Chalidocean, which lay to the eastern edge of the central province, some twenty-five miles

from the sea. The Atlantean continent was flat in the
north and inclined to be dry, although it was by no
means barren. Most of the mountain ranges lay to the
south and although it would be rash to equate any of
today's land masses with remnants of the Atlantean
continent, because the topography changed so drasti-
cally at the time of the axis tilt, the topmost peaks
roughly coincide with the islands of the Azores.

The Atlanteans were, on the whole, a fair-skinned
race and tall by present standards. They were a handsome people even by modern criteria. Men and women
were equal in Atlantis and were not assessed by their
physique or even their intellectual ability but by their
spiritual evolution. People lived comparatively simple
lives. They did not work in factories, although they did
manufacture goods. Many were the trades an individual
could pursue if he was not destined for the priesthood.
There was little manual work other than that done in the
fields, where crops were sown and reaped.

Although there was no telecommunication in the
modern sense, the Atlanteans were in several ways
more advanced than people are today. They had no cars
or telephones or television because they did not need
them. Messages were sent telepathically from temple to
temple; many of the priests could levitate themselves
and there was not the need for speed that is so prevalent
today. All heavy construction was done sonically;
houses, temples and other buildings were erected by
means of sonic gongs which were tuned to the pitch of
the substance being used. The gong was struck and, by
prolonging the note and controlling the tone, huge
blocks of stone could be raised or lowered without the
aid of machinery or human labour. Heat and power
were supplied by solar energy.

The Atlanteans were a kindly people, but not very
good at dealing with the aggression of less advanced
communities. Their major weakness was their tendency

to be too philosophical. The ideal state for humanity is only achieved by a nice balance between the spiritual and the material. Any nation or community which drifts too far either way will come to grief. The Atlanteans became so spiritual and philosophically-minded, that when trouble came they had no idea how to meet it and were overwhelmed.

As time went by, the Atlantean priesthood became more and more withdrawn. They began to abstain from normal living and to practise celibacy. The gap between them and the ordinary people widened and gradually they became less and less aware of what was happening to their charges. People came from less evolved lands and started to take an interest in the strange powers possessed by this handsome race. In due course many of the immigrants intermarried with the more evolved Atlanteans and as the evolutionary strain deteriorated, the less evolved began to learn some of the occult secrets that had helped to lift Atlantis to greatness. But they had neither the wisdom nor evolution to control the forces with which they were tampering, and gradually the practice of black magic spread across the country.

The uncorrupted priests tried hard to fight their adversaries, but as is often the case when good men come up against bad, it is the latter who win because the former are limited to clean methods of defence. Ordinary folk were intimidated by renegade priests, hideous orgies took place, parents sacrificed their children out of fear. All the key evolutionary events affecting the destiny of a planet are known in the higher spheres even before that planet comes into existence. So it was with Atlantis, and the temporary loss of this great continent was to prove one of the most serious retrogressions the Earth has ever experienced.

The seasons passed and strange signs began to appear in the skies—signs which meant much to the high priests. Earthquakes occurred, volcanoes erupted. Fear spread throughout a strangely tense continent. On instructions from the priesthood small bands of Atlanteans set out in every direction. As the final days approached the reigning Arcanophus summoned all the powers used by the priesthood on the Atlantean vibration. By means of certain rituals he sealed those rays so that none could call upon them until the time came when there would once more be people incarnate on Earth of a similar evolutionary vibration to the sealer himself. The key to this seal he placed in the land you call England. Its symbol is the sword of St. Michael, or the Excalibur of Arthur, and its withdrawal signifies the emergence of the new Atlantean race.*

Part of the teaching of H-A revolves around the fact that Atlantis did not fulfil its karma. At the height of the havoc on the continent, when the planet Lucifer was drawn into the Earth's orbit, the upheavals caused the Earth's axis to tilt and Atlantis sank beneath the waves, taking with it a vital spiritual quality; a quality that needs to be brought back. It is on this very specific, yet subtle, wavelength that the Atlantean society works and which it recognises in H-A. It is a vibration which they feel will go forward as part of the transition into the Aquarian age.

The Atlanteans, however, are adamant that this affinity with Atlantis does not indicate that they live in the past. On a symbolic level they have come together to work out their individual and collective karma; they know they have been together before. But this knowledge is relevant only where it applies to the present time and to the current stage of their own and the planet's evolution. Although David and Diane, in particular, link with their past quite

---

* The New Age generally, not merely the Atlanteans as a group.

strongly and recollect aspects of lives in Atlantis, the Atlanteans do not advocate that people delve into past incarnations unless for a specific therapeutic purpose. In fact, they generally discourage the exercise which they say can be unbalancing and misleading.

Knowledge of an isolated previous life, even if it were accurate, could give a very distorted emphasis to the present life because it would be one life experience taken out of many tens or hundreds. Having said that, however, a particular problem in this life might be greatly helped if trauma in a previous life were mentally re-experienced and possible karmic conditions appreciated. A spirit comes into a physical body at any one time to conceptualise what that life might offer as a complement to the experience it has had throughout its history. When we incarnate in a physical body, we bring with us the essence of all we are and have been. We are the sum total of all we have ever experienced. It is all here with us, in the now.

H-A warned the Atlanteans that "if they did not get on with it soon, it would be too late." He said he had given them all the information he felt he could give: it was now up to them. It was also around this time that H-A proposed another change of symbol. The ankh and the sun had represented the balance between the positive and negative, Osiris and Isis, the Christos and Sophia. It had been vital to try to find a point of balance between the two; between the giving out and go-aheadness of the sun, and the love, compassion and understanding of the ankh. The Atlanteans had gained a great deal from the influence of this symbol; it had brought a calmness, a vibration of love to the society.

Now, said H-A, they had reached the stage at which they had earned the right to add a third aspect, so that once again the Atlanteans could take a new step forward. This new symbol would retain the determination and rugged impulse which in the first years had helped to bring the society through; it would still carry the love and compassion and out-going influences of the sun and ankh. But it would now absorb a third influence.

Eventually, on H-A's advice, the society decided to incorporate the symbol of the equidistant cross within a circle, opening up the Atlanteans to a more universal relevance. This, said H-A, would give them the necessary impulse to enter the subtle struggle involved in bringing light to "this beautiful planet." It would lead the society firmly into the Aquarian age, establishing it in a positive way. This third aspect which complements the sun and ankh, is a symbol of the Aquarian age, explained H-A, yet also one that goes back to the earliest times of man on this planet. In the centre of the symbol is the centre of all things, and at the points are the four elements. The circle of light surrounding it brings together the spiritual and the material.

The ankh and the sun were to remain, placed within the new equidistant cross and the circle. The Atlanteans would therefore still encompass the balance between the positive and negative but, in addition, the society would acquire the direction it needed to use the wisdom it was accumulating, and also the dedication to help its fellow beings. The symbol, representing Michael or the planet itself, would offer a sense of completeness and provide another stepping stone towards the future.

Signalling the end of an era, the Atlanteans heard that the area around their headquarters in St. George's Street was to be sold and redeveloped. Beset with financial problems, in any case, the society decided to sell Isis House. And finally, in 1979, the three families began in earnest to look for a large country property that would suit them all. H-A had already told them that the place they would find was, in a sense, prepared for them, and had been eons ago. It was a centre of light which would attract and help people; a source of healing energy and spiritual power. This was how they visualised it in their meditations, without any material detail.

On H-A's information they knew that the property was on high ground, had its own spring, was surrounded by trees and on the periphery of a small town. It was the most beautiful place, he told them, and he was excited by it. But more than that he was not going to say; he would not tell them exactly where it was. It was up to them to be alert and quick to recognise it when it came. They had to make their own decision.

As commonplace as H-A's description might sound, the families searched in vain for nearly two years. They viewed as many as ten properties, each person tuning in individually to see how it felt to them. But none fitted all the required categories. For example, Henley who still had two years to teach at Wynstones, could not move too far away, and in any case the children were also at school there. When a feature of a property was inappropriate, "a powerful shutter came down to stop us going wrong," says David. In that way they always felt guided and protected, but after two years they began to feel concern; nothing seemed to be consolidating for them.

With a project as important as finding a community from which they hoped a spiritual impulse would spring, surely they could ask for H-A's help? In frustration Tony decided to do a trance and they asked H-A, "What on earth is going on?" Couldn't H-A give them some other help? In a typical kind of reply, H-A suggested that perhaps they were not going about things in the right way. On reflection they realised this was true. Instead of dealing with ten exasperated estate agents, perhaps they should do something more direct.

In the winter of 1980 Ann put a one-paragraph advertisement in the *Sunday Times*, appealing for a country house or complex within a fifteen mile radius of Gloucester. The response was immediate. A business man was selling Runnings Park in West Malvern which, according to the woman who phoned them, had great possibilities. Ann went to view. Immediately she felt that it was a marvellous place and ideal for their purpose. She was totally convinced, however, when just as she was leaving "a great heron flew over the middle of the house and out down the valley." She felt sure this was an omen. In ancient Egyptian mythology the Ibis (Thoth) symbolises karma, and the heron is the English version of the Ibis. When the others saw it later all agreed with Ann that Runnings Park was ideal—apart from Tony, that is. Usually so intuitive, Tony had no strong feelings whatever about the property and simply agreed to accept whatever the others decided.

Runnings Park was so much better than the Atlanteans had ever dreamed it could be. They had been prepared to take over an old school or hospital, anything that would house them properly, serve their needs and suit their pockets. Here at Runnings Park, however, was a crop of buildings, ideal for community living, but extensive enough for separate family homes. They knew without doubt they had to purchase the property. There was just one problem; they could not afford to! They had worked with the notion of raising a certain sum, but the owner, a tough-dealing millionaire, was asking nearly double, and insisted that the contract be signed on a certain date.

Everything has a 'right' time, but as H-A says, since we have free will and choices are in our hands, we can also *make* it the right time. By making a commitment to do something we set up the patterns in the ether and thereby send it on its way. True to this rule, Tricia and Henley had put their house on the market and it had sold quickly. They had put their furniture in store and were living with friends. They could put down the deposit, but what about the rest? In fact the ideal solution was right under their noses. The Furlongs' partners at Highfield House, Judy and Mick Jewell, planned in time to move somewhere close by. Instead, they were invited to join the enterprise.

Together the four families could just manage to raise the necessary capital and a price was agreed. Then, within a

Mick and Judy Jewell

few days of signing the contract, the vendor informed them that many years earlier he had promised first refusal, if ever he wished to sell the property, to a London business man. He had only just remembered, but—and it was a vital but—he did not want this man to have it! The following days were agonising, but in the end the owner bought the business man out of the running, selling off some of the land to do so.

The drama was still not over, however. Literally days before completion was due on the sale of Highfield House, the prospective buyers backed out. It was put back on the market as two separate units, and while the Furlongs sold their part in three months it took the Jewells a year to sell their's. When the original sale fell through the two families had to raise in a fortnight a bridging loan of £80,000 to complete the purchase of Runnings Park. By any stretch of the imagination this wasn't easy, says Diane, but they managed it by changing to a more sympathetic bank. In the event between them they lost £10,000.

H-A had warned them that there would be difficulties; they had no idea quite what a struggle it would be. Yet, in July 1981 the four couples moved into Runnings Park. At last the long-held vision of being part of a 'family of Atlanteans' was realised.

PART THREE

Earthing the Spirit

Runnings Park

Chapter Seven

Doing it Themselves

"It is all in my teachings" said Helio-Arcanophus. "I have given you everything you need to know. Now you must apply the philosophy to yourselves." H-A has never spoon-fed the Atlanteans. He has always indicated that they should unearth meaning and experience for themselves and learn from it in the process. Yet, in the heady days of the psychic, they did lean heavily on H-A. Whenever problems arose, invariably the consensus would be "Let's have a trance". They expected to be given instructions and in those days they were.

Now, at Runnings Park, the true meaning of H-A's words became apparent. The group was thrown back far more on its own resources. H-A had shadowed them closely to see them make this vital step, and although he has never left them, he certainly stepped back during that first difficult year. If any one of them was really stuck he was accessible, but he was not permanently 'on the telephone line'. From now on they must begin to trust their own inspiration and try to find a path to their own higher selves, the teacher within. They knew their outer work could not go beyond the level they had reached within themselves at any one moment.

Psychism can take you so far, says H-A, but the inner growth of spiritual understanding is the real key. Spiritual evolution is not something mysterious. It is not perceiving colours you cannot see with the physical eyes; it is not out-of-body experiences. Finding spirituality is growing in understanding and that understanding has to come right down to the physical and material level. In this sense, H-A emphasised that self-responsibility is the clue to the process.

The transition from the Piscean to the Aquarian Age, like all transitions, is a painful experience because it represents change. This change is difficult for mankind and yet terribly important for those who are concerned with helping and guiding planet Earth, for they must bring their influence to bear in a way that does not deny the free will to which all living beings, to a greater or lesser degree are entitled.

The greatest gift that mankind possesses is that quality of free will, yet it is the most difficult facet of personality and character to handle. All the time you are placing the fruit just beyond your reach and there is never a certainty that you will find it. You have to find your own route to that fruit and it is part of your experience and karma that you should do so. Sometimes, when it seems far away, those moments of inadequacy seem to swell and can so easily consume you, devour you until you turn to face yourself.

When you look at the problems of inner development you cannot escape from the fact that all inner and outer development is a question of self-responsibility, self-motivation and self-will. You can never control another's destiny because for each one of you on this planet, absolute self-responsibility is a predominant factor. But so often man does not recognise or want to recognise that fact. On the one hand he wants to influence other people's decisions, on the other hand he finds it much easier to blame another or look for a reason outside himself for his own inadequacies, instead of facing that which is within, simple and obvious.

The universe as such, is simple; it is mankind who tries to see it in a complicated way. And the universe is made up of universes, all of them comparable, all of them part of the whole, the microcosm within the macrocosm. All forms of experience are thought creations from the Godhead. You choose your body. You have chosen the type of physical life that you are at present undergoing and you have the free will to progress that life. What could be simpler than that? You have the same free will to turn experience in on yourself and cause you worry and distress. It is your own choice, your own responsibility. Herein lies the key to the unfoldment of the human psyche.

The group knew that to achieve the unfoldment of their inner understanding they would have to plumb and confront the psychological depths within themselves. Coming to Runnings Park demanded that they all—eight adults of widely varying ages* and temperaments—begin to look at themselves with total honesty, even though this was something they thought they had already been doing. Over the years they had each been involved in healing, and in teaching spiritual truths they had taken positions of leadership at numerous seminars and courses. Yet, here at Runnings Park, it was glaringly obvious that there were areas of their own personalities that still had to be integrated and brought into harmony with the whole. It was a truly traumatic experience for them all and an enormous challenge. It was as though the place itself represented a giant mirror. It revealed their innermost selves and highlighted their problems, their strengths and weaknesses so acutely that no one in the group could escape its relentless gaze.

---

* Tony: 56 Henley: 54 David: 38 Mick: 40
  Ann: 57 Tricia: 46 Diane: 36 Judy: 34

The first task was domestic reorganisation, which took almost two years. Originally designed as a handsome, timbered dairy farm and, more recently, an extensive family house with stables, the Runnings Park complex had to be restructured into suitable, separate living units. All the families had adjoining sections around three sides of an inner courtyard garden. Each section had its inconveniences as well as advantages. The Neates, for example, had a huge lounge with plenty of room for Ann's piano— but no bedrooms, kitchen or bathroom. The Furlongs had a spacious kitchen and dining room, but no bedrooms or lounge. The Thomases had a fine master bedroom and lounge but no kitchen. The Jewells had bedrooms and a bathroom but no decent kitchen or lounge. There was much exhausting extension work to be carried out.

At the same time, bedrooms had to be built on the fourth side of the courtyard, converting what had once been the dairy and other undeveloped farm buildings into a hotel and conference centre. If Runnings Park was to succeed, it had to develop into some sort of communal business and this was an ideal way of making a commercial living. David, as the most talented and experienced in design and building, was instrumental in the architectural design of the whole area and responsible for its development. The group also elected him to be manager and this, for David was where the troubles began. Runnings Park was different from an ordinary business, in that they were all involved and all living there. There were numerous meetings and endless decisions to be made. With four families living in such close proximity they were obviously forced to balance the needs of the company against the needs of the individual families. In addition, everyone had his own views about what was required of Runnings Park itself and the way the business needed to be run.

However, since David as manager was in the position of having a large say over what happened, he felt he had a strong perception of what needed to be done. He was young and prepared to take risks: Highfield House had, after all, been most adventurous. His was principally the energy that moved them forward more quickly than the older members might have wished, and he became frustrated when the others wanted to slow things down. His major lesson has been to learn patience. "One of the things I resented and had to come to terms with was, as I saw it, Tony and Henley's parental attitude towards what I was doing."

Invariably, when problems erupted they manifested as irritation against other individuals. This, in turn, forced each of them to turn the mirror to themselves and say "Why do I have this problem? What is it in me that is creating it?" Everyone, it seems, had their own particular crisis to overcome. To begin with, Henley, who was deeply anxious about whether or not the project was going to work, felt surprisingly sad about leaving the cottage in Stroud in which he and Tricia had invested so much love and care. And because they suddenly found they were no longer 'kings in their own domain', no longer in control of their own environment, it was a difficult beginning. "Decisions were made even though sometimes one was not in agreement. We went ahead just the same, for the good of the project."

In addition, Henley was committed to two more years of teaching at Wynstones, which meant travelling back and forth, twenty-seven miles each way every day. As much as anything he was concerned about the effect this had on the four older children who were also still at the school. (The younger four, Maaten and Claire Furlong and Simon and Sharon Jewell, now went to local schools.) What is more, he was still deeply entrenched in the whole ethos of Steiner education and therefore could not participate fully in Runnings Park. "Things were happening and moving on without me playing a proper part. Although I tried to help in a practical way, for two years it was difficult to integrate with what was going on."

The fact that Henley was teaching at Wynstones, obviously placed a heavier burden on Tricia. Not only did she have to organise her own home, but because she has always loved cooking, it was assumed she would take on the job of hotel cook. This she did virtually single-handed until eventually, in December 1983, they could afford to employ some mid-week help. Living in this day-to-day way, Tricia realised she was not as emotionally strong as she thought she was. She felt that the creative, sensitive side of her nature was "a delicate seed that needed time to emerge", and deep down she knew this seed would flower into something special for her. But in the confusion of the new undertaking, "those who were being strong and forthright did not understand that they were drawing on that vulnerable seed."

Diane, too, had her own cross to bear. The Furlong's house was at the end of the courtyard closest to the hotel, so while the hotel was being completed, their kitchen and lounge were temporarily put at the disposal of hotel guests. The Atlantean and hotel office was also there. As a result, for almost a year the family was crammed into one small, as yet undecorated part of the house and Diane found she had limited access to her own kitchen. "I found it very difficult to share. Whenever I walked in, Uncle Tom Cobleigh and all were sitting there having deep conversations," she says. "It was as though it didn't belong to me at all."

The pain was excruciating, she says. With her rising sign in Cancer her home is extremely important to her. Here she felt she was living in a goldfish bowl. One day she had finally 'had enough'. She fled to the hotel sauna which adjoins their house, threatening to take the car key and leave. David managed to hide her glasses and, being very short-sighted, this gave her breathing space! In the end she decided instead to ask Ann for healing, and through the technique of guided imagery, she was able to understand what was happening to her.

In her imagination she saw her 'castle', her home, being smashed to pieces by a large tree growing alongside. To resolve the situation she uprooted the tree, planted another one, and then began to rebuild the castle brick by brick. Ann helped her every day for a fortnight and she continued her meditation for many weeks after that. But it took her a year to feel really well again. David, in the meantime, arranged for the next part of the hotel to be built more quickly. She says the experience taught her that she must learn to say no, and that it is permissible for her to do so. Also, that it is acceptable for people to use her home, but on her terms.

Perhaps here it should be explained that although Judy and Mick Jewell are not so deeply involved in the Atlantean work, they are nonetheless a vital and respected component of Runnings Park. It is almost as though they were pulled in by the destiny of the others, particularly David and Diane through their experience at Highfield House. Judy and Mick provide an important balance of thought and activity, particularly Mick since he is the most practical, down-to-earth character in this scenario. He immediately turned his attention to the land and to the animals which he loves and he spends as much time in this way as his daily work as site foreman in the building trade allows.

However, Mick has never expressed interest in the spiritual aspect of the Atlanteans, and although in coming to Runnings Park he obviously had his own challenges to face, perhaps for him it represented less of an inner struggle. Judy plays a far more obvious role within the group, both in the running of the domestic side of the hotel and as a healer. She has been through her own kind of trauma in making the transition.

Ann, on the other hand, experienced her worst 'low' before she moved to Runnings Park. This mid-life crisis, during which she lost weight to below seven stone and worried everyone around her, helped her to understand herself much better and also to relate to others in a way she had not found possible before. As her children reached their teens, their emotional upheavals uncovered her own deep-seated anger which she had to learn to let go. A disruptive, fiery side of her personality emerged, opposing the part that loves singing and dancing, peace and harmony. This anger, she finally realised was an inverted use of a valuable 'power' within her. By using its 'laser-like beam' in healing, particularly that of a more occult nature, it could be released constructively. It was useful, she feels, to have sorted out these difficulties before the group came together, otherwise she knows she would have found it much more difficult to adjust.

The greatest crisis for Tony, as it had always been, was the dichotomy in his life between accepting and rejecting himself as a medium. The responsibility of this work and the ever-present possibility that he could bring through ideas that were coloured by his own attitude continued to concern him. As H-A says, no philosophy or teaching can be one hundred per cent accurate because whatever the source of wisdom it has to come through the medium of the physical brain of man, consciously or unconsciously.

In fact, it is only in the last two years, after much soul-searching and heartache and coming to terms with 'so many shadows', that Tony has been able to accept fully the course of his life. In his attempts to cope with the two opposing forces: "one where you begin to think you are someone important, and the other where you tear yourself to pieces thinking you are nothing", he has at last understood what is perhaps H-A's most urgent message: to accept himself and to *be* himself. The key to life is *acceptance*.

> It sounds simple to say "continually reassess yourself and see yourself for what you are, no more, no less", but because of the subtle and wrongful influences around this planet people become frightened to look at themselves. They become frightened of failure and they

feel a sense of inadequacy. They feel they cannot cope. This really is the heart of the problem.

No one need feel inadequate, and the very first step to understanding yourself, to understanding your fellow men, the whole planet and all the problems therein and thereon, is to *accept*. It is, however, very easy to roll the word *accept* off the end of your tongue, but it is another thing to understand what it means in depth. It means that whatever happens in your life, whatever external influences surround you, you must stop, look at yourself and see yourself honestly for what you are. There is nothing to be ashamed of or to feel guilty about, because you are all spirits experiencing through a physical body and evolving towards an all-loving Godhead. If you were perfect you would not be here.

You must learn to accept yourself despite all your failings and faults and realise that you are a spirit of God, a thought of God who created you and gave you free will. Drink in the wondrous experience of just being part of this magnificent universe. Understand it in its full glory and then you will begin to see that all these other problems that seem to press in on you in your daily life are petty and unimportant, compared with the real essence of beingness moving towards the divine, pure, all-wise Light.

How are you going to achieve this acceptance? You don't have to do anything mysterious, but you do have to be prepared to make the effort and to remember that every effort you make in spiritual seeking will always be rewarded. Acceptance means more than just looking at yourself and saying "I wasn't very clever over this, was I?" and "I am rather pleased that I did that." Such thoughts are part of acceptance, but there is something more to it than that. Imagine that you are standing on a certain rung of the ladder of evolution—your own personal ladder unrelated to those of others—and say to yourself: *"This is me, this is where I stand. In order to go forward I am going to accept. I accept myself and I accept God and all things for a few seconds without question."* By saying this you will raise yourself into a spiritual state that is beyond analysis.

You cannot start to move upwards until you accept both yourself as you are and your neighbour as he is. Acceptance does not mean looking at yourself as a psychological problem, because you are not a psychological problem. You are a loving thought of God and it is sad to see people torturing themselves because they cannot find a picture that suits them. They are not allowing themselves to sit back and realise that spiritual acceptance means putting their faith into something, trusting God, trusting a higher force to guide them. Man in his material seeking has lost sight of this simple spiritual truth.

When you accept this with your hearts and minds open, not blind but open, you will be surprised, you will suddenly feel comforted because you will be enabling the spirit world to help you. Then you will start to move forward: you will begin to find attunement, which is the next step. This is the starting point of the search for fulfillment through the path of spiritual evolution.

It seems to Tony that the true spiritual path is a hard one, and you can only come through at the cost of your own personal pain. "A part of H-A's philosophy that is meaningful to me is that God does not cause men to suffer; it is man who causes his own suffering. Sometimes when I look at the agony I have gone through, I see how needless it was, how I could have chosen an easier way. But H-A had made it clear that we have complete free will, and we choose how to run our lives. We experience in the light of our own stage of evolution."

Evolution involves reaching a state of consciousness wherein you realise you no longer need to undergo an experience, where you can say to yourself "I understand that now. I can see why it had to happen. I totally accept it." One of the hardest realisations is that there are no short cuts in the process of evolution. It is an individual path along which a spirit gains sufficient experience of physical life in order to learn the lessons of acceptance, love and wisdom and to find a balance and harmony within itself and in relation to all other life.

Reading all the esoteric books that have ever been published will not help you one scrap unless you are really prepared within yourself to make the effort in your everyday living, in your relationships with other people and in the decisions you make that affect those around you. Putting it in a humorous vein, the day you can sit in your car and smile when someone tries to hurry you on or flashes his lights at you with impatience, will be the day you have learned a lesson in acceptance!

The process of evolving is assisted by recognising all experiences as something you can utilize and accept. There is no such thing as bad experience; the only thing that can be bad about it is your attitude towards it. God is a god of love, a god of understanding and compassion. Life is a means of providing physical manifestation and experience for the spirit; it is for you to handle that experience. There are those who believe that the path of spirituality lies in the so-called esoteric mysteries. But all the esoteric mysteries in this universe are within you: each one of you has your own tower of mysteries that can be as simple or as complex as you choose to make it.

In an ideal sense, physical life is beautiful because that beneficent Godhead has given you the free will to make your own decisions as to how you live your life. Yes, you are limited by your physical body; you are limited by the environmental conditions in which you live but, even allowing for those limitations, you have the free will to move about inside that environment. You are the master of your own destiny.

Physical life is not only beautiful, it is a unique experience for the spirit. It is not always easy for a spirit to handle the physical body, especially in this day and age, but life is a form of experience it cannot undergo in any other way. Your physical bodies are a combination of chemicals that react to your thought. If something alarming happens and you feel a sense of fear, then it means that various chemicals are reacting in your body to stimulate it. Your senses are heightened and your reactions become faster to help you to cope with the emergency that has arisen. It is a very real experience. Yet fear is an illusion. It is an emotion of the body and not of the spirit. The closer the relationship of your spirit to your physical body, the more it will enable you to rise above physical emotions such as fear. It is important to learn how to make the optimum use of your emotional nature, not allowing it to dissipate through negative reactions, but using it in a positive and beneficial way through love and joy.

Each time you incarnate your spirit brings with it the sum total of all its prior experiences. You are what you have made yourself at any one given moment in time. You are making your own life pattern by your thoughts. Your actions are of course the product of your thoughts and your challenge in life is to cope with all the various problems and situations you meet. It is no good sitting back and saying to yourself "I am what I am, this is how God made me, people must accept me as I am." You cannot get away with that because God did not make you that way, you made yourself. You are fashioning yourself at this very moment. You cannot push responsibility on to anyone else, it is yours alone. On the other hand, you should never be frightened of failure because failure is only a state of mind. All experience is valuable and relevant and much can be learned from a mistake or failure.

You need to be more objective in your understanding of yourself, to find a balance between negating yourself on the one hand, and on the other hand, over-expressing yourself to make other people think you are a person of substance or that, without you, a situation will crumble. There is no such situation and it may be that without you events would take a different course that would be better for others. Egoism is a trap for even the most wary. Unbridled ego always inhibits evolution.

It is easy to feel critical of someone else, to feel you can do better, or conversely, to feel a sense of inferiority that everyone else can do better than you. Both these lines of thinking are out of balance. They are unbalanced because they forget that thoughts affect that other person. Perhaps it is your fault that the other person is doing it wrong in your eyes.

What others think of you is unimportant; it is their concern and not yours. Never at any time do things for effect, but do them only for a purpose. When it comes to the moment of reckoning the only judge will be yourself. Learn to understand your own relationship with those around you. Learn to respect and love those around you and to extend this love and respect to animals, plants and all forms of life, because all are thoughts of God experiencing in their own particular way as part of the whole experience.

You are each playing a vital role in the evolution of this planet because everything you do, think and say is not only affecting the thoughts of everyone else around you but of every being on this planet, in the solar system, in the galaxy and in the universe. All is one. You are here to find that oneness through harmony and balance both within yourself and in your relationship with the universe.

The problems of living together, of facing each other, and accepting each other proved such a struggle that at times they wondered whether it was all worth the effort. H-A had told them they would go through difficulties, but they had laughed when he said there would be occasions when they would almost hate each other! "Sometimes I think we have been very poor pupils", says Henley. "H-A's wisdom and understanding of our predicament has made us feel very inadequate at times."

Not least of their challenges and their biggest act of faith, was money. Although H-A implied that they should not feel overwhelmed by the financial worries and that these would eventually sort themselves out, there were times when individually and collectively, they were on the brink of financial collapse. The hotel had to generate sufficient income for Diane, who had taken on all the secretarial work, as well as David, Tricia and Judy. Frequently the situation was such that David, who was responsible for the finances, could not be paid.

Yet, deep down through their understanding of the philosophy they knew there was always an inner area to work out any challenges and doubts. And, as difficult as it was, the process of integration was also fascinating and exciting. "It was rather like being married to seven people," says David. It extended them beyond their wildest predictions, and as Tricia adds, "the spirit was willing, but the flesh turned out to be pretty weak!"

Somehow, however, these eight totally different, strong-willed characters managed to establish relationships, both within themselves and between each other, and learned in the process to express what they felt with love and kindness. Although all responsibility for a balanced community must be shared because there is no community figurehead and consequently no cocoon of comfort to sink back into, they nonetheless learned to co-operate harmoniously. They reached levels of tolerance they would never have imagined.

No one could be envious of the personal struggles they have had, says Henley. If you stand back from it all, he says, it was an extraordinary thing to undertake. "People thought we were extremely brave, throwing up security to live in this way with other people. But security of this kind has never meant much to us. What does have meaning is a spiritual security, and that only comes inasmuch as you can believe that what you are doing is your destiny in this life."

It is this absolute certainty that has ultimately kept them together. On the spiritual plane, where they know each other so well, their rapport and the "extraordinary feeling" they can sometimes generate between them in meditation and healing is unquestionable. When the going was really tough they trusted that basic miracle. Also, one of the main attributes that has kept them going, says Tricia, is being able to laugh at themselves and what they are handling. "To be over-sanctimonious would be unbearable. Those who get too 'precious' might have fallen by the wayside."

Coming to Runnings Park was a shock to them all. "Most people might take a few years to go through one aspect of their personality," says Diane. "I feel we packed about three incarnations into our first three years, which made us sort ourselves out in a very quickened way." But today they are closer as a group than they have ever been. Their overriding concern is to work together and to bring out as many strengths in each other as possible. Wanting to help and support each other creates a clearer, purer link between them. Where before they were reluctant to acknowledge the sacrifice they were making and grasped tightly on to their own survival mechanisms, now they feel they can drop their outer coats and look at each other truthfully.

H-A has indicated that future problems will make this particular period seem like the kindergarten! But the difficulties they face next will be related to helping the planet, on an inner and outer level. The greatest *personal* trauma any of them will undergo in this life was in coming to Runnings Park. This demanded, on an initiatory level, a great deal of self-sacrifice and was one of the hardest to face.

The situation is continually changing and adapting; they will always be growing. Each family had retreated at one stage or another, wanting to guard their own piece of territory in the old way, and pull up the drawbridge of their own particular castle. But at last they were ready to come back, to create a true community. For almost four years they had been dealing with their destiny as individuals and as a group and learning to cope as the energies of Runnings Park increased. "From the earliest days H-A has based his philosophy on love, tolerance, understanding and humility," says Tricia. He has made clear that whatever we embark on, the fuel for that activity comes from the energies expressed in those words. If we cannot live these qualities ourselves, we cannot pronounce them to others. It is a very simple understanding and code of ethics, which is why H-A's teaching is not world-shattering, but has changed a lot of people's lives."

If this group of people was setting up a centre of light, others would turn towards them to see what they were doing, would ask what was different about Runnings Park, and who were the people involved. If they themselves did not learn to cope with these kinds of challenges and to harmonise their different personalities, then they would have no real strength. They needed a firm foundation on which to build a truly spiritual centre.

Chapter Eight

Finding the Path

Helio-Arcanophus says that his teaching can be heard and understood on many different levels. It is up to each individual to extract its essence and intuit what it is saying to him personally. The philosophy has never been insular, but has served as a springboard, an encouragement for people to open out, to pursue their own interests and extend their own particular talents. Consequently, once the practical chores involved with the reorganising of Runnings Park had levelled off, each member of the group was released once again to look at various aspects of the teaching in the way they 'heard' it for themselves.

Tony had always cherished the idea that when they had discovered their spiritual home and founded a community, he would be able to relinquish the material side of his life. He saw himself as a 'monk', devoting the rest of his life to spiritual aspiration. On the contrary, however, when he came to Runnings Park he was plunged even deeper into commercial life. At that time Dr Alec Forbes was helping to set up the Cancer Help Centre in Bristol and required the purest vitamins, minerals and enzymes to prescribe for his patients. Since he knew Tony had once owned a health food shop and was currently acting as an agent for a US vitamin manufacturer, he asked him whether he could consider the idea of manufacturing a whole new concept in hypoallergenic vitamins and minerals. Non-toxic binders, bio-availability and absorption were of utmost importance.

Tony felt that this was beyond his capability but he spoke of it to a friend, Eric Llewellyn. Eric, who had been in the vitamin and mineral field and had worked for Rodale as sales manager, had had a passionate interest in nutrition and the quality of food since he first became a confirmed vegetarian twenty years ago. He and Tony first met when Eric visited the Cheltenham health food shop and noticed an ankh on sale in the craft section. He was struck by this as he had been interested in spiritual matters for some years, and it sparked off a conversation. Eventually he joined the Atlanteans. Eric was fired with enthusiasm by Dr Forbes' idea: he was as obsessive as Tony about high standards and quality products. He also knew enough about vitamin manufacture to find the right technical people to produce them, so together he and Tony started *Nature's Own*.

Because of his innate ambivalence to the psychic work, Tony perhaps more than anyone has kept the feet of the Atlanteans society on the ground. His marketing training at Shell, not only gave him the experience of running an organisation, but also established an objectivity about psychism and spirituality. As H-A says, the difficulty that mankind faces is trying to find a balance between spiritual seeking and achievement with commercial and economic standards.

Most people would probably consider that money is evil, that money causes anger, feuds and wars. But is it the money or is it the greed that motivates the way in which the money is used? There is nothing unethical or wrong with material achievement itself. It *can* lead to a sense of fulfilment and social responsibility, but just as often it carries misfortune and unhappiness in its wake, and it increases the danger of losing one's balance and perspective.

Wealth is often considered immoral, especially by those who are unable to attain it themselves! But money is an energy; it is a means of exchange. It is a means of convenience so that energy can be exchanged. It is the abuse of money that is evil and the abuse of money comes through greed and fear, fear of what might happen if you haven't got it. Some feel that everyone should have the same amount of money and others feel a very different way, but this is because money has become an object in itself rather than a means of exchange. Well-earned material achievements such as financial success and possessions do not weight the scales against you when you leave your physical body. The trouble lies not in the material success itself, but in the way you might live your life after you have won it. This is not to suggest you should immediately give it away. Only if that wealth were acquired unscrupulously or used harmfully could it be considered evil.

If by working harder than others or by using special skills you become wealthy, then it is for you to live your life as you see fit. If you wish to use your money to help people less fortunate than yourself in a way that helps them to evolve and not merely enables them to live off your riches—say, by donating money for healing or education—then you are doing something useful. How you handle your success or wealth will naturally reflect your spiritual status. If a man who has amassed great wealth gives it away because he fears what might happen to him if he does not do so, he has not assisted his spiritual progress. He has tried to be what he cannot be, for fear of what he might become if not. This is not meant to be a conundrum. So many people in the world today are frightened and cannot accept themselves as they are. They accept neither their own limitations nor their own possibilities, as they aspire to be either what they are not, or how they wish other people to see them.

Not until man throws aside this false identity and sees himself as he is, will a human society based on real values emerge. A time will come when material possessions such as those you prize today will be worthless. Money and its power will become things of the past, and man will achieve a spiritual maturity which will bring with it an entirely new set of values.

As a founder member of the Atlanteans and the medium through whom most of the teachings have come, Tony is often called upon as the society's spokesman. Also, since the Atlanteans are non-partisan and it is widely accepted that Tony is able to look to the greater good of the whole, he has become involved in several initiatives to spread the authority of the holistic health movement. As well as being a trustee of the Wrekin Trust, Chairman of Wynstones School and a member of the council of the College of Psychic Studies in London, Tony is a member of the Holistic Council for Cancer, set up in in 1983 to establish ethics and standards for practitioners in the holistic treatment of cancer and other diseases. Related to that, he is Trustee and Vice-Chairman of ANAC, the Association for New Approaches to Cancer, which categorises the different cancer centres and support groups and spearheads the holistic approach to cancer in England. On the inspiration of Alec Forbes at Bristol, Tony also helped to organise and motivate the Cheltenham Cancer Help Centre, housed at the Cotswold Natural Health Centre in Cheltenham. As Henley says, "Tony is the sort of man who inspires invitations of this kind!"

The Cotswold Natural Health Centre was, in fact, originally David's inspiration. It grew out of an educational idea he had in 1978 to bridge the gap between allopathic and alternative medicine. At first he ran lectures at Highfield House and then he hired a lecture hall once a month. Finally he rented a house in Cheltenham as a centre where, by letting out rooms to various practitioners, people could experience the therapies as well as learn about them. Through this, David was active in setting up the Natural Health Network, again under the inspiration of Dr Forbes. Until he came to Runnings Park he served as Chairman of the committee of both these organisations.

To help pay for the Cotswold Centre, *Nature's Own* occupied the basement and ground floor of the house and in 1983 the Cancer Help Centre was opened in Cheltenham, closely linked to Bristol. They were fortunate in having Dr John Cosh, a retired consultant rheumatologist and heart specialist from Bath, who was a friend and fellow-Atlantean and now a neighbour at Runnings Park, to be the Medical Director of the Centre. With the necessary vitamins and minerals already on the premises and with Ann, and later Tricia, available to assume the role of counsellor/healer, they had sufficient experienced personnel to proceed. The centre ran successfully for two years until the premises were no longer available, but it is hoped that it will continue again some time in the future in the Malvern area.

Counselling is a gift that Ann especially has decided to develop and Tricia, too, although she has not yet "taken the bull by the horns in a big way". As the Atlanteans have evolved, so their approach to healing has changed. It was no longer just a matter of asking the client about his problem and "giving five or six minutes of healing energy". They realised they were required to offer something more. At first, says Ann, a healer wants to emulate an ordinary doctor and make the person better. But healers need continually to be working on themselves and they soon reach the stage where they understand that the optimum is not to cure but to heal, and that is a very different thing. As H-A says, although we speak of a sufferer being healed, what the healer is actually doing is assisting the patient to heal himself. A healer is a person who is a suitable channel for cosmic power which, when directed by thought to the etheric body of a sufferer, aids the patient's own spirit to make the necessary adjustment.

There is far more to healing than effecting an improvement or negation of the symptoms, says Ann. Certainly that is an important aspect, but healing is a rebalancing process, helping the patient to rise above the condition. People need to be helped to discover the reasons for their problems, to be persuaded to face themselves truthfully and, above all, to learn to love and accept themselves. Again, it is a matter of self-responsibility. "Healing should take place on all levels: spiritual, emotional, mental and physical," she says. "It might in fact be karmically the allotted time for a person to pass from this life, but we would like to feel he had died healed, meaning that he had truly come to terms with himself and his illness."

Often a person links into a severe illness for a karmic reason; it may be an unconscious wish to atone for some past action or a deliberate decision to experience and grow through that illness. If the healer can help the person to understand this, the latter may then reach an inner realisation whereby he no longer needs the illness. "The healer has no right to make a judgement, only to help the client towards experiencing an inner understanding and acceptance that can sometimes effect a release."

> The quality of all psychic work on this planet has changed, and healing itself is also changing as the healers become more aware of different values that need to be achieved by their healing. As interest in healing grows, so do the healers grow, and they become aware that healing is truly about harmony and balance on all levels of being. After all, this is what the Godhead is about: perfect harmony. As the healers become more awakened, so they become conscious of the need to help their clients to grow through their problem and to help them to extend their consciousness.
>
> If you consider the significance of the holistic

approach to treating disease, no longer are people just looking to effect a cure, but to use their talents to improve the quality of life, the quality of death. What they really mean by that is an expansion of the consciousness. When you hear counsellors talking about people dying healed, what they mean is that the person's spirit has left the physical shell in an illuminated and enlightened fashion. So that when they come back to another life they can bring that illumination and enlightenment with them and maybe teach and help others to reach that level of consciousness. So healing is developing, but so is the whole approach to man helping man.

This more holistic approach to healing, then, requires that ideally healers also become counsellors, and for cancer clients in particular this is extremely important. As Ann explains, when a person has a life-threatening disease like cancer, they are in a very unique state of mind. They feel they are absolutely 'up against it' and are usually open to the possibility of facing a big change in their lives. Centres like those at Bristol and Cheltenham are helping people to accept that there may be areas of their lives in which there are blockages, whether spiritual, mental or emotional, and that they are a whole being, not just a physical body. This kind of work is extremely challenging to a counsellor who needs to understand the client as rapidly and as deeply as possible in order to catalyse for them something that can gradually unfold.

When the Atlanteans headquarters came to Runnings Park, it was important once again to find a symbol to represent the change, this emerging wholeness. To begin with they contemplated changing the name of the society completely. 'The Atlanteans' had been appropriate when the emphasis of the society was on psychic work and the obvious link with Atlantis. Now, perhaps, the name resonated too much with the past. Besides that, Runnings

Park was more than simply the headquarters and spiritual home of the society. It extended far beyond the Atlanteans.

In the end, however, they decided not to abandon the old name because it meant a great deal to many of its members. They felt a kinship with the ideas and were committed to be part of what, under that name, they represented. H-A has talked about an 'umbrella of protection' and when people join the society they elect to come under the overall free will umbrella of that spiritual philosophy on an Atlantean vibration, which is something specific, unmistakable and obviously stems from H-A. When they make a connection with the group a measure of that vibration 'glances off' and something seems to fall into place within them. It engenders a deep affiliation.

The Atlanteans are an open-ended, totally non-sectarian society, and there is no room for dogma. The society helps people to find and express themselves in a way that is uniquely right for them. Many current members have taken the philosophy out into the world, instigating new initiatives in the community, in adult education and complementary medicine, for example. They wield considerable influence in their chosen field of work; not necessarily in terms of numbers, but by being there at the right time for the right people. It is a 'get up and go' philosophy, not a passive one.

Finally they decided to establish a separate, more commercial arm of the society. It was important, they felt, to make the venture pay in order to encourage New Age activities from which so many people obviously benefit. This exoteric side of the society, which would present itself to the world through courses, books and cassettes, was to be known as *Pegasus*. Tony had dreamed of the winged horse on the night of New Year's Eve 1980 when they had first decided to change the name. It is a powerful symbol representing the spiritualisation of the lower energies and the transformation of evil into good. The more esoteric work of sending out healing in a concentrated way to bring love and light and understanding to difficult situations, would remain with the Atlanteans. This includes the recent setting up of an Atlantean Esoteric School, to give a deeper understanding of the universe in a more intellectual way to those who have reached a stage of consciousness at which they feel they are ready for something more profound.

In 1983 when Henley left Wynstones, it was he who, as treasurer of the Atlantean society, became full-time organiser and promoter of Pegasus activities. These include residential weekend workshops on healing, growth of awareness and meditation run by themselves, or on related subjects by other New Age groups: astrology, psychology, stress, outward bound, reflexology, sound and movement. Business courses and conferences held during the week ensure that the wider public also benefits from the energies at Runnings Park.

One of the most exciting innovations has been the founding of the College of Healing, a joint venture with other healers and doctors. Its Principal is Hertha Larive, a well-respected healer and spiritual teacher who trained at the late Ronald Beasley's College of Psycho-therapeutics. The three-part diploma course, each part lasting a week, (taken over not less than a year) offers a deep level of understanding and education in healing, but also concentrates on helping its pupils to expand their own spiritual consciousness. Five of the resident Atlanteans teach at the College, while Henley for the moment prefers to work as administrator.

The question that should be paramount in the minds of any spiritually-seeking person, says H-A, is 'How can I optimise my life? How can I gain most from it and, in gaining the most from it, help my fellow beings?'; because the type of experience we undergo in the physical body is one in which we need to relate to and harmonize with others in order to gain from our experience.

Helio-Arcanophus suggests that it is our responsibility to find the direction and purpose of our life, and our responsibility to fulfil it. No one can tell us what it is or how to do it, for it is something that we have to seek and find for ourselves. It is up to us to see that our lives are meaningful and purposeful, to try to understand ourselves and those around us, to strive to understand life and its portent. We have the free will to accept or refuse to do this. This is the very first challenge of life, he says. When you have found it, something inside you tells you that you have clicked into place.

David, who has always been interested in geometry and maps, has found that leylines (lines of cosmic force across the planet) and earth energies are a fascinating study. Runnings Park sits in special relationship to the Malvern Hills, which in turn lie in special relationship to certain energy patterns throughout Britain. The hills in fact have been a source of revelation and wonder to them all. Their beauty, their expansiveness, their power as a land feature and on a deeper, earth energy level, have been a constant inspiration.

Power accumulates for different reasons. As the planet evolved, a number of civilisations emerged, each with its own type of culture and power. From an esoteric point of view these powers accumulate with each successive generation. For example, if you were to set aside a small room in your house for purely psychic use, you would find that in time an atmosphere would build up: the power generated in that room would accumulate and make its presence felt. When you do spiritual or psychic work you create a spiral of energy with its own force field, which exists over several 'octaves', and gradually it builds up until it begins to have a life of its own.

You invite a friend to your room, perhaps to do some healing, then you introduce a third person and you all carry out psychic work together. All this time the power inside your room is increasing. You have started a power centre. This, then, is the way that certain power centres have evolved, by means of the energy accumulated over many years and in some cases, centuries, in one place. Stonehenge is a perfect example of such a centre, although it was later misused and has now fallen into disuse.

Strong thought patterns imprinted in the earth can cause an imbalance. Throughout history, David explains, many events have happened on the planet, not all beautiful. Tuning into a power centre, or even just into the earth, it is possible to trigger a disturbed level where something unpleasant has happened in the past. For example, a friend of the Furlongs had had a bad accident in his home and although he was being treated by a homoeopath did not seem to improve. When on request Diane tuned into his house she 'saw' people wrapped in shawls, weeping in the darkness. She felt bowed down with sadness and pain, and became aware that she was seeing a path leading out of London at the time of the Black Death. People were escaping the plague, carrying their sorrow with them. This path went straight through the house and the tears and heartache were deeply embedded in the earth beneath it. Dramatic confirmation of this vision came when their friend said that the homoeopath had prescribed bourbon for him, the homoeopathic treatment for bubonic plague! Healing to the earth was subsequently carried out to correct this imbalance. There are other types of power centres which originated thousands of years ago.

Our predecessors learned how to manipulate highly potent occult forces and possibly the greatest and most powerful of these dynasties flourished in Atlantis. Before Atlantis sank, many were forewarned of the coming disaster. They also knew that the power they had accumulated over the centuries would retain its potency if it were correctly sealed in suitable locations, and a protection placed around them lest anyone stumble on them by accident.

At the time of the fall of Atlantis, a number of power centres were placed in various parts of the world, not the least of which are those hidden in England. This country will have the *opportunity* to play an important part in future world affairs, not in the field of politics or warfare, but as a pathfinder in the struggle to achieve sanity and balance. England has far from reached such a goal and there is a grave danger that it might even veer in the opposite direction, but it is hoped that, as time goes by, the right groups will gradually begin to tap these power centres and use the energies they release to benefit humanity and the world at large. These sites hold the accumulated power of centuries. Unleashed they can be extremely dangerous to the uninitiated. Releasing power you are hopelessly ill-equipped to control could destroy not only yourself, but bring suffering and ruin on countless others. The story of Pandora's box is, like so many others, no idle myth.

There is great responsibility involved. This is not a game, nor an achievement, it is a sacred responsibility to mankind. Such powers are not for aggressive use or for self-aggrandisement, but for dispensing light and love and power to arrest the evil that is rampant in the world. Discovering these power centres is something you must find out for yourselves, either individually or in groups. As you progress you begin to see and as you reach higher levels you begin to understand. That understanding might lead you to one power centre which will in due course lead you to the next. But before you embark on this path, you must be confident that you are equal to the task, that your motives are utterly selfless and that you are capable of handling whatever it is you find behind each successive sealed door.

These centres do not exist in haphazard fashion, but form a pattern linked by thought lines, so that each site must be considered in relation to the overall complex. No two centres are identical, each one performs a unique function. Many occultists recognise that they exist in certain groupings and endeavour to find the key to the group so that they may harness the energy of that complex as a whole.

The thought patterns behind power centres exist on all levels and are intercommunicative, so if someone is to make most use of a centre, he must first learn to understand its many facets or frequencies. There are now many people who are interested in the study of earth energies. In David's experience, if they tune into a sacred site and do not understand what they are doing, disturbing things can happen, sometimes resulting in illness. It requires a certain understanding and discipline to be able to work with and help Earth at this level. Yet, with the right keys and the right attitude it is possible to link into this energy and use it to bring balance and healing throughout the planet. David and Diane, especially, are involved in this kind of research work. They lecture on leyline networks, earth energies and sacred sites and, along with others, try to help the polarity of the leys. As H-A originally told the group, there are untapped energies at Runnings Park which the six have since been able to harness for their own work for the planet.

It may take years to achieve the degree of understanding necessary to undertake work in this particular field and then, only if you are able to tune in to the frequency of those who originally planted the centres, will you be able to discover and tap them. Each power centre is a miniature universe in itself, a pulsating living vortex of energy which, if treated and nurtured correctly can help to bring love, reassurance and healing to the

The Furlongs, the Thomases, the Neates and the Jewells

world. But used improperly it can be a dangerous weapon. All forms of energy are neither good nor evil in themselves; it is the use to which they are put that determines their shade. The difference between good and evil is in the intention. You either want to help someone or you want to harm them; you choose to be selfless or selfish, to create or destroy. If used for good, the power waiting to be tapped at these sources could generate peace and tolerance among the peoples of the world.

H-A, say the Atlanteans, steers but never compels. He asks everyone to find his own way:

> All experience is self-realised and, indeed, the whole process of evolution is self-realisation, whether that applies to man himself or to the planet as a whole with all the many kinds of experience and evolution taking place on it and within it. Because of this process of unfoldment, there can be no complete understanding at any one moment of evolution, only a partial understanding of the whole. In other words, a being can only be what it is, no more and no less, at any one moment in time. There is nothing wrong or negative in this state of incompletion. It is a wonderful state to be in for you are all the time experiencing and learning in a universe which is infinite. You will go on for ever and ever, for life is eternal. It is the process of eternally growing and evolving.

In that sense, anything that anyone can do to bring harmony and balance, no matter how simple, helps the whole. Just trying to be conscious about our own lives affects the broader canvas. It is service at every level. Each of us must do what we can.

Chapter Nine

A Way of Life

In 1983 an exciting new development was that Diane began to 'take' Helio-Arcanophus. She had somehow known she would many years before. Although in essence the transmissions are the same, there is a slightly different flavour because she and Tony are very different channels. To Diane "it is as though H-A walks in from the left, into my vision: it is as though I step to one side. It is not a take-over, but more than anything a shift of my consciousness. People who know me know it isn't me because I couldn't talk with such fluency on such subjects."

Diane believes that her way of working is less dangerous than going into trance. It is unnecessary for her to eject her spirit out of her body and to a certain extent she remains conscious of what is happening. Recently H-A commented that spirit communication is moving away from aspects of trance mediumship into the more telepathic forms of communication more in keeping with the mental age of Aquarius. Originally Tony worked only through deep trance, but he has gradually moved away from this to the lighter form of telepathic trance that Diane uses. It is a linking through the subtle levels of consciousness to the higher self and beyond to the finer levels of wisdom and understanding. Since H-A himself is a specific level of inspiration, you could call it a specific wavelength.

Diane also feels that H-A links down through her higher

self. When she finds there is no time to prepare a lecture in advance, for example, she simply puts out thoughts to H-A and asks that she tell the audience what is right for them (which from the experience of the author works with astonishing success). "In my imagination I see myself going into my higher self and opening up channels. It's like a crutch in a way: without that ability I can't take my place in the scheme of things." But in allowing that to happen, she says, her understanding and knowledge have increased. "I'm hearing what is said and I'm learning from myself. Sometimes it is coming from an outside entity like H-A, and sometimes from my higher self linking into the vast ocean of knowledge."

All six find now that they are learning to attune through their higher selves when teaching or lecturing and receive inspiration as they talk.

Experience in a physical body is not complete without some development of the more sensitive aspects of yourself. You all know for yourselves that when you come together with others the atmosphere of a room is heightened. It is heightened in one respect, but made more difficult in another, because to gain the most from that heightened energy you have to find an attunement with those around you. Attunement is not compromise, but an absolute acceptance of each other. Some think that acceptance means sacrifice, a popular misconception in spiritual seeking. But sacrifice is not a necessary part of evolution. True attunement requires awareness and through awareness comes acceptance. It requires being able to lift yourself above the emotional states associated with experience in the physical body and find an attunement that exists on a spiritual level.

The spirit does not have emotions but, of the higher emotions, one could say that compassion most nearly expresses attunement; not sentiment, but a compassionate attunement of your spirit with another spirit, a complete awareness of that other spirit, not expecting it or anticipating it to be anything other than what it is. It is what it is, because that spirit, like you, is the sum total of all its previous experience. One of the greatest challenges in life is to find this attunement when you come together with others through a deep level of awareness and acceptance.

How can you find this optimum experience and allow your higher nature to manifest more positively? There is a part of you not within the physical shell, but near. Many call this the 'higher self', for it is that part of you which is in communication with the higher realms of the universe. Through gaining attunement with your higher self you will also gradually become more aware of your guardian angel or guide, that spirit which decides of its own free will to stay with you throughout your life, to help and guide you along your journey in a physical body.

Attuning to the higher self is not achieved without a certain amount of hard work. It has to be tackled in a very discerning way because, when one starts to operate on these levels, there are just as many temptations, misconceptions, charlatans and negative thoughts as there are in physical life. In fact there are more! It is important to remember that for every step you take along the spiritual path, you need to take three steps towards working on your own character. In order to handle the higher energies, you must be aware of and constantly rebalance your own inner energies. Spiritual philosophy needs to be put into practise and not just talked about; it is for everyday life and everyday relationships. So in starting to seek for your higher self—not the other side of your personality, but the higher aspect of your being—you need to tread carefully and with discrimination. It is advisable to gain experience in the basic techniques of meditation, learning to focus your mind and create a disciplined framework, before attempting to find an awareness of this other aspect of your being.*

Gaining contact with this other aspect of your own being through meditation is only the first step, for you need then to learn to harmonise with it and this may take much longer to achieve. But if you persevere you will begin to experience in a way that you have never experienced before within the limitations and confines of an earthly body. Through learning to contact your guide you will also obtain much help, using the archetypal images as they present themselves to you in meditation to find answers to situations, to help the world around you and the planet as a whole.

But a word of warning. When dealing with this level of sensitivity and communication, your motivation and your requests must only be self*less*, that which does not promise you the attainment of personal power or give you any form of advantage over any other being, or you will reap karmic rebound through the universal law of cause and effect. The benefits are infinite, but so are the dangers. Use what you experience wisely as a means of expanding your own awareness, your own compassion and acceptance of others, your own love of all things.

It had taken Diane six years to come to terms with all that was happening to her, but suddenly it was as though a key had been turned inside her, particularly when H-A acknowledged her as a medium for his teaching. Her challenge, she says, is to trust in H-A's wisdom that she is worthy of the responsibility of being at Runnings Park. "I like to think he understands I'm still growing and understanding and coming to terms with a feeling deep

---

* The basic Atlantean approach to meditation is expounded clearly in *Meditation. A Basic Course in Three Parts*, published by The Atlanteans.

within me, that I have the ability to carry it out and won't be tested too much! I am always staggered when I read or listen to what I bring through from H-A, that it is so concise, that it was able to happen. It is not like a 'high', but a feeling of job satisfaction I suppose. It has certainly helped me, given me a lot of confidence, that there is a way I can contribute that I can do well."

As Diane says, when you make your dedication to the powers of light, it is one thing to "do it in your head", but quite another to follow your commitment through. We create our own hurdles, put our own fences up and establish the pace at which we wish to go. We think we should do better and drive ourselves harder through our own inner need. H-A says there is no easy answer to spiritual understanding. It takes hard work and determination. The most important task in life is to find our inner melody, harmony and love, so that when we face the adversities of physical life we do not allow ourselves to be torn apart and are no longer afraid. There are no short cuts, only difficulty and hardship. We have freedom of expression, freedom of self-responsibility and freedom to make mistakes.

The most important contribution we can make at any one time is to keep our own life disciplined and in balance and to try to live every aspect fully and consciously, looking at ordinary life as a spiritual education. Their own process demanded that the group should come to terms with everyday life and bring their spiritual qualities down to a practical level. The way to God, says H-A, is not through introversion; it is no good seeking within if you do not also look without. He stresses that balance means accepting and understanding simple material things as well as spiritual seeking. Balance is not maintained by shutting things out of life as taboo, but by accepting them and then making a choice freely. A thing may be bad for us, but we cannot rise above it by ignoring it and pretending it does not exist. We can only overcome it by accepting it, so that we no longer need to be affected by it.

When asked about television, for example, H-A told them that the overall influence is not particularly good. To begin with, there is a certain radius outside which you should sit because any closer the rays can be harmful. In addition there are programmes that are not conducive to the spiritual life or for the healthy growth of children. He also said there would develop a kind of music that would jar the psyche. However, the Runnings Park children, like any other, watch Top of the Pops!

Lifestyle, then, is a question of balance. None of those at Runnings Park smoke, from choice, but all will occasionally take a drink, although never before psychic work or healing. They were taught early on that more than a very small quantity of alcohol loosens the conscious control between the spirit and the physical brain and is therefore detrimental to disciplined psychism. They eat whole food wherever possible and have been mostly vegetarian for many years. H-A made it clear that for reasons of karma, ethics, economy *and* good health— physical, emotional and spiritual—a vegetarian diet is an ideal to work towards.

Eventually all mankind will become vegetarians, but this is looking many, many years ahead. If you want to become vegetarian do so by all means: but remember that man has been carnivorous for a long while. A complete abstinence from any form of flesh may cause a lack of balance in your body, even to the point at which your health begins to deteriorate, for each of your bodily needs will vary somewhat. If this the case—and if prescribed vitamin supplements and other elements fail to restore full health—it may be advisable to abandon being wholly vegetarian. It may well be that in this incarnation you are not ready to take this step. You might, for instance, include fish in your diet, or one of the 'lighter' meats such as chicken.

However, terrible suffering is inflicted on millions of animals and other creatures every day in order to produce food, especially fear at the moment of death, and you may well find that your health, digestion and energy levels will considerably improve if you begin to eat less meat or do without it altogether. But it is entirely a personal matter, a step to be taken in accordance with your own understanding or conscience and the conditions of your body. People involved in any kind of sensitive or healing work should abstain from animal meat as it increases the density of the body from a psychic point of view and this can impede your dealings with the inner planes and subtle bodies.

It does not necessarily follow that a vegetarian is a better person than a meat eater. A man could be utterly unscrupulous, even evil, and yet be a vegetarian, as history has already demonstrated. Another person could be a meat eater and lead an exemplary life. So do not think of vegetarianism either as a sacrifice or as something that is going to improve you spiritually. Ask yourself simply, "Am I ready for it yet?" It is true that plants and other vegetation have responses of their own. But the day is far distant when human beings will no longer need to ingest other living organisms. Until then, enjoy the rich variety of foods that the planet has produced for you and, if you will, occasionally remember to thank the living things you eat in order to survive. They make the sacrifice willingly.

For the core group of the Atlanteans, six individuals with different interests and methods who, from totally dissimilar backgrounds, had very little in common, and who admit that in other circumstances would probably not have come together, the philosophy itself has been the great balancer, the absolute leveller in their lives at

Runnings Park. It gives them a uniquely fresh approach to life, a wider and broader canvas on which to work. Each family creates a family structure, but not to the detriment of the other individuals concerned. There is respect for each other, knowing that everyone contributes a valid and important part to the whole. And that includes the children. They all believe that the Rudolf Steiner education has stimulated a sensitivity in their children. As H-A says, education is a spiritual process, not only involving the ability to absorb knowledge, but also the wisdom to apply what is learned.

A certain amount of learning must be undertaken and there is much of great wonder and interest to be read and understood, but it is wrong for it to be absorbed in a mechanical fashion. It has become almost like a competition to see how much knowledge can be absorbed, how many books can be read. There are many people who can quote from the great philosophies that have been written, but who when asked what *they* think, will give an evasive answer which means nothing. Knowledge for its own sake can be limiting and even dangerous if it is not partnered with wisdom.

Many cases of juvenile imbalance can be partly attributed to the fact that young people are not under the guidance of those who necessarily understand what they are teaching. They can be trained to pass the required examinations, but are they taught by teachers of real understanding? Thousands of years ago in Atlantis, the teachers were people who had a vocational 'calling' and whose spirits were of suitable evolution for the work. While a child was still young its parents would take it to the temple and there it was decided to which profession it would be most suited. Those selected for teaching were then trained in the temple by men and women of great understanding, wisdom and intelligence.

The small child was taught gradually, for any form of sudden cramming is bad. It was also taught about the ordinary things of life as well as the more intellectual subjects and, instead of learning parrot-fashion, it was encouraged in its own creative thinking. This is very necessary if the child is going to teach others later in its life, for it is not sufficient merely to refer to books as the teachers of today tend to do. To be able to say "I can tell you from my own experience because I have done this and can show you", is a great asset, although it would be impossible of course to experience all one learns.

A teacher is really born not made, for true teaching ability cannot be acquired by passing the necessary examinations. Some people can be guided to become good teachers, but there is something lacking in their training which impedes their progress as leaders able to inspire their charges. Education, then, is more than a word which merely means the amount of knowledge a person can acquire. If you learn to respect your fellow men for their wisdom rather than for their knowledge, your spiritual gains will be greater, and, where education is concerned, the ideal state to aim for is a balanced one in which academic knowledge and wisdom walk hand in hand.

The work of the parents has obviously affected the Runnings Park children. Once the older ones reached the age of ten, they were encouraged to take part in the festivals. But by twelve or thirteen, they tended to rebel and since then have been allowed to develop their own spiritual ideas, and not persuaded into an Atlantean approach. Semira Neate, the oldest at twenty-one, attended Wynstones but decided against higher education. She has a natural acumen for business and has found a niche working at *Nature's Own*. She was the first to leave home. Deri Thomas, twenty-one and working for a degree in sports studies at Sheffield Polytechnic, has enjoyed living at Runnings Park but is rather anxious about the whole project—he wants it to succeed. Yet when Henley and Tricia offered to explain more about what they were doing as Atlanteans, he replied that one day he might like to hear but "now I'm not quite ready."

Dominic Neate and Katie Thomas (both nineteen) were born in the Chinese year of the firehorse, which occurs only every sixty years. In the old days Chinese people tried to avoid having children in that year! Both are extremely talented young people who struggle with their temperaments. Dominic, nearing the end of school at Wynstones, loves Runnings Park, but at times has resented the commitment his family has made. At this stage in life Katie, who is taking 'A' level English, theatre studies and art history at Hereford College of Art, finds the atmosphere of Runnings Park too insular. She is sensitive (if impatient at times) to the difficulties, both financial and physical, that her parents have had to face in these early years, and often wonders if it has been worth it!

The Furlongs, Maaten, 13, and Claire, 14, have taken events very much in their stride, although sometimes they would have liked more attention from their parents. Like Maaten and Claire, Simon, 15, and Sharon, 13, Jewell have now become accustomed to the lack of privacy and enjoy the facilities available to them at Runnings Park. They appreciate the friendly atmosphere. No one knows what the Atlanteans will mean to them all in the long run: obviously they do not yet understand the karmic implications. Inevitably they will try out other viewpoints and make their own choices from their own free will.

Those who live at Runnings Park greatly appreciate the beauty that surrounds them, nourishing their understanding of the other kingdoms of nature. Soon they intend to cultivate an organic kitchen garden to grow their own food. Since so much of modern living is unhealthy, H-A has said he would like them to aim for self-sufficiency. Eating a lettuce or carrot, for example, that has had its metabolism changed by artificial chemicals, by over or under-fertilised soil, by the artificial environment in which it has been raised, causes the overall sustenance to be out of balance often resulting in malnutrition for the consumer. Moreover, H-A has suggested they uncover their own water supply. They have always felt that the pond in the courtyard has a special quality of energy, and when it came to considering where to build a sanctuary for meditation, David had the inspiration to place it in the centre of the courtyard, halfway over the pond at the place where a natural spring flowed in. In time they will attempt to unearth the two remaining natural springs.

They also have plans to landscape the bottom lake, to create a healing garden and to plant an orchard in an effort to create harmony within their environment and to engender in others a consciousness of the link between kingdoms. As H-A says, if man's evolution is going to continue forward on this planet he needs to establish a rapport with other forms of existence. He has to be able to see himself, not only for what he is as an individual, but how he fits into the cosmic picture as a whole: and not just a casual appreciation, but with deep awareness on all levels: intellectual, emotional and physical, so that his ideas and actions are guided by the needs of the whole. But perhaps above all, Runnings Park will endeavour to transmit an atmosphere of love, which as H-A says is the perfect synthesis of wisdom, power and intelligence.

Love is the ultimate energy, embracing and sustaining all others. It is the fuel that drives the wheels of nature, the current running through the machinery of the universes, both physical and subtle. Remove it, even for an instant, and the entire cosmos would collapse.

To experience life fully you must give and receive, so that a flow is created, using the terms 'give' and 'receive' in the broadest possible sense. To become complete you have to give love and receive it; you have to give understanding and receive it; you have to give help and receive it; and so forth, on every level. If you do one without the other, an imbalance is created. If you take all the time but never give, you become a miser, not necessarily in the monetary sense, but maybe a spiritual or emotional miser. Or you can go to the other extreme: you can go about blindly giving here, there and everywhere, advertising your lack of inner strength, your hunger for love and attention. It is difficult to say which of the two is a sadder sight.

When you have experienced the healing and exhilarating power of love—and by 'love' is meant something more majestic than the assortment of selfish emotions that often masquerade as love—when you have felt the extraordinary benefits of giving *and* receiving love, begin to release some of this power, not only to your own circle of loved ones but also to your fellow beings, known and unknown, making sure that you do not leave out the animal, plant and mineral kingdoms who serve so unselfishly. Birds, animals, trees, flowers, minerals, rivers, seas, even the air itself, all these different manifestations of life need your care and understanding. To deny any of them is to impoverish yourself and others around you.

There is no more important message than to learn to love and co-exist with nature. Have you ever felt the tremendous strength and power of a tree? The evolution of trees is quite different from your own; it is a complementary form of spiritual growth. Trees can give you far more than oxygen, building materials and fuel. When you are feeling spiritually low, mentally depressed and unable to cope with life and all its shocks and adversities, go and stand against a really big tree, not just any tree, because some will be more in tune with you than others. Experiment, and you will soon find the one that is right for you: as you stand against it or lie in its shadow your whole body will begin to relax and be filled with a sense of well-being. You will have started to benefit from nature by attuning to one of its primary forces.

Plants, flowers and herbs can also give you more than you ever imagined. These gifts should neither be demanded nor stolen, but exchanged: exchanged with your kindness, care and co-operation. The nature kingdoms are overwhelmed with sadness at the way man has desecrated so much of the earth. When, however, a man does achieve a harmony and friendship with nature, you can immediately sense this in him, as it gives him a kind of serenity, a settled and kindly approach to life. Do all in your power, then, in whatever way you are able, to restore the balance between yourselves and the ever-patient, endlessly generous planetary Being who sustains you. Is not her patience and her generosity—despite your appalling cruelty to her—the ultimate proof of her love?

As Tricia suggests, this group's belief and understanding of a spiritual ideal is like a growing child. The couples are working together for the good of the whole, but within that they must experience their own spiritual growth. They are a multifaceted jewel and because of the make-up of the group there are always many ways of looking at everything they do. Provided they aim for balance and each knows he or she is expressing what they have incarnated to express, and that this is never fixed, the greater is the influence as each shines out into the environment.

In the last years H-A has become very close to each person individually. It is as though he is overseeing them. If there is anything he feels they ought to do, he may overshadow one of them in meditation. Or they may just recognise his nudging through inspiration and intuitively understand his wishes. It works in different ways. H-A himself has said he would like to move more closely to them, so that they can merge with him. But he cannot force, he cannot stipulate. His 'role' he says is changing all the time.

Whenever any spirit of light commits itself to helping a group, whoever, whatever, however they may be, it will always be there so long as that group needs it. These people could move from me, but I will always be there.

The six see the pattern of the group behind them and around them. They do not have a clear idea of what lies ahead of them. As Tricia says, whenever you are setting up anything new and acting as a pioneer there can be great leaps forward. The next step, when you are no longer pioneering, is far more difficult: you just have to get on. "In spite of the days when one is down and there is a feeling of defeat at some level, we all have the faith it will work out. We see the limitless possibilities, but can only take one step at a time. That's what makes it interesting." H-A himself has suggested that the group is moving into a new phase. When they first came to Runnings Park they had really to find each other and find themselves. Now, he says, their opportunity to expand and move forward has become much greater. The challenge is to see whether or not they can achieve it. His love and encouragement, he says, are always there.

"Picking up H-A has provided some of the real highlights of my life," says Tony. "What is important is the feeling of love, warmth, compassion, humility and gentleness. On the one or two occasions when it has been on a truly high level the experience was so moving, so subtle, so beautiful that I felt I wanted to burst, to leave my body and go towards that vibration and never come back. The thing that impresses me most is the tremendous understanding of people and situations H-A has. He never claims to be anything or anybody; he has always taken the view that the philosophy should be judged on content. The outstanding aspect of the teaching is that it is not to raise the ego, but only to raise the consciousness."

For his part, H-A says it is a great privilege to work with this group of people, trying to help them find themselves. Difficult at times, he says, but it becomes very beautiful to watch because not only do the individual flowers begin to blossom, but also the flowerbed begins to assume a harmony and structure. Just as you would walk into a garden and say "Isn't this beautiful" because of the subtle relationship of colours, smells, shape and sizes, this says H-A is how he sees not only the team at Runnings Park but also the many others involved in the Atlanteans who are just as much part of the whole.

The Atlanteans as a group has been slow to mature, suggests Tony. Perhaps because it allows its followers a great deal of liberty and does not try to force them into any form of rigid dogma. Yet this slowness has also augmented the inner resources of stability and strength, gradually generating unseen and undreamed of energies that enable the group always to be searching for and finding new depths of spiritual wonder and higher awareness.

"The society has always been the sum of the people involved rather than a solid mass following an unbending principle," says Tony. "For many years we have meandered, trying to find ourselves. We may still be searching but I feel strongly that we have found our direction. A much greater harmony and understanding is developing within the society. Never before have the various branches and groups around the country proffered such a will to work together, while standing on their own feet and developing their own understanding of the whole. I expect a great expansion of Atlantean awareness and consciousness in the next five years. We have gained respect as a group, let us now justify that confidence."

Towards the end of 1984 a new share structure was introduced at Runnings Park which invited close friends to participate financially in the project. In March 1985 the stable block was converted into hotel bedrooms and the extra income generated assured the financial stability of Runnings Park. A new conference room to be completed in 1986 rounds off a phase of rebuilding which began when the four families moved to Runnings Park.

As Ann says, now that the foundations for the future have been well laid—the spirit has been grounded in matter—the way is paved for the next stage of spiritual growth. Having established their roots and drawn sustenance and support from their ability to grow through their relationships with each other, they now feel sufficiently strong to emerge into the wider world, to expand and give out their love and strength. "It is an ever-creative expansion," says Ann. "And it is this that seems to act as a catalyst for the growing potential of others. It has been a long haul to reach this stage of unfoldment, but I feel privileged to be part of it."

More and more people are applying for courses and returning again and again. They are coming to know Runnings Park as a centre of light that is contributing to the emergence of the Aquarian impulse. All healers are working ultimately towards the same thing, to help the planet and its people to find balance and harmony. The Atlanteans' role is part of that complete jigsaw. Their hope and vision is that Runnings Park will become an even brighter light on the landscape, helping people to find wholeness within and to spread that wholeness and light around the planet.

As Tricia says, with H-A's gentle guidance from above and much hard work, harrowing moments and profound happiness below, Runnings Park now has a purpose on many levels. People who come can choose to accept it in various ways: as hotel guest, visitor, conference delegate, patient, healer or student of universal truth. "I don't believe we are unique in what we have done," she says. "Our kind of project can be set up by anybody if they so

Henley and Tricia   David and Diane   Ann and Tony

choose. Our uniqueness is why we have done it and how! Our hope for the future is to pass on to as many as care to listen, the spiritual essence that not only reached us, but touched us and flowed through us. We are the sum total of what we have listened to, learned and put into practice. We do not wish to keep it to ourselves."

Runnings Park has been created as a firm, solid base from which the Atlanteans can work. The peace and energy of the place will give them the strength they need to carry out the tasks before them. "What those tasks are I have no idea," says Diane. "But with the love and guidance from H-A I hope that we will all be sensitive to the next steps and that we are able to fulfil that which is right for all of us, and for the planet and mankind as a whole."

As Henley says, you just go on developing and gaining experience. There is no goal, just more exploring. In the end it is 'knowing'; knowing that if you turned your back on it all you would regret it. "The important thing is to feel of real service; to people, and perhaps to the world. It is standing on your own feet, learning from those around you, but knowing that what you are doing is right and being prepared to stand by what you know is right. It is speaking on the level of humanness that we all share."

PART FOUR

Transformation

Runnings Park with the Malvern Hills behind

Chapter Ten

And Now

When Helio-Arcanophus first approached The Atlanteans, he could only give to that group of people what they were ready to receive from him. Today, while providing the same essence, the same principles, the same truth, H-A will teach the Atlanteans in accordance with their present level of understanding. As they have matured and grown with him, he has been able to offer a maturity in the philosophy. This, says H-A, is important for any teaching, whether a religion such as Christianity or Buddhism, or an esoteric group. No esoteric teaching should ever be static. It must be evolving and moving all the time, as each one of us is evolving all the time. It is a story of development.

One problem today is that after the initiator of a philosophy has moved on, the people who follow find it difficult to allow themselves to expand. Partly due to the influence of the Piscean age, too many spiritual teachings have become locked and unable to move forward. The advent of the new solar age, the Aquarian Age, is the moment when man's imagination, man's creativity, man's opportunity to truly take on new spiritual dimensions is going to take place. As H-A explains, although there is nothing that he said in the early days of The Atlanteans that he necessarily totally disagrees with now, he is looking at the same truth and offering it from a slightly broader perspective. H-A has come to this planet to communicate through various sensitives in accordance with the needs of life today.

Earlier spiritual teachings were, in their way, far more dogmatic. Going back to Moses and the Ten Commandments, the same cosmic law was seen from a narrower perspective and did not allow man the luxury of thinking about and working out his own karma. It had to be specific and dictatorial: 'an eye for an eye', 'thou shalt and thou shalt not', based more on fear than on love.

As time passed, two extremes in religious thought developed. One, the hidden mysteries of the secret orders, and the other, the open forms of spiritual belief such as Buddhism and Confucianism. Nearly 2,000 years ago the spirit of God came into the physical body of a Jew named Jesus. Jesus' spirit came from the Ultimate, but it was housed in a human body and, although the link between spirit and the conscious mind was strong, he had to make his own decisions and resolve his own karma. This was one of the first changes in direction, where the full free will of the spirit of man was allowed to manifest in a more expansive way.

In his teaching, says H-A, he has tried with gentleness and understanding to advance mystical thought; to move beyond existing pantheons and their limited concepts. The motivation behind The Atlanteans is one of peace, tolerance, love and acceptance. The teaching is practical and yet esoteric and therefore encompasses a wide spectrum of understanding. On the practical side there is the day-to-day healing and meditation techniques, built on solid foundations: so grounded that some might say the society lacks a spiritual dimension in its basic meditation course. But, as H-A says, unless we can come to terms with physical and material experience on this earth, the spiritual does not mean anything.

His teachings are a way of life, a philosophy of cosmic

lore which is being put forth into the world to help people to see themselves as they are, to see others as they are and to see the universe as it is. He has tried to tackle the more philosophical aspects which encourage each individual to become a free thinker, responsible for his own destiny. We are reaching a stage, he says, where man is beginning to acknowledge and accept his own divinity, his own responsibility to recognise that divinity within him, to move forward towards discovering and exercising free will, to search every corner of his own karma and to find the right answer and a perspective for his own life.

Long ago a wise man said 'Man, know thyself'.* Who am I to pretend to have a better formula? In these three words lie all the answers to your problems, from the personal to the global. Investigate yourself, and what do you find? That you are a synthesis of all creation, of all kingdoms, both physical and subtle. You are *energy*. You are *matter*: atoms, molecules, cells, organs, all in constant motion. You are *mineral*: your body contains a high proportion of minerals, chemical and trace elements. You are *water*: almost all water; was not the sea the laboratory from which you first emerged? You are *vegetable*: in your hair and nails, for instance. You are *animal*: armed with weapons of attack and defence, and a body with which to explore and manipulate your surroundings. You are *human*: the midway point or fulcrum of all life, a synthesis of all the energies and impulses both higher and lower. You are *emotion*: a useful system of overdrive that extends your feelings and demands counterbalance. You are *mind* and *intelligence*: which is your spacecraft, your infinity machine. You are *will*: a fantastic weapon, which can help you achieve the near impossible, or if misused.... You are *spirit*: part of which is with you here on Earth, while

---

* Socrates

part remains in the higher worlds. You are *love*: the light within you that you hide or shield or allow to illuminate everything around you.

Combine all these and you *are* God, co-creator in the great experiment. Exactly how you convert this information into the unfolding plan of your life must remain for you yourselves to decide. No one can and no one will drop all the answers into your lap, for such would be to break the universal law. But here is a clue, and one that should not be overlooked: *do not dismiss the simple or obvious*. You love to complicate. You love to go the long and hard way round. In your thought and philosophy and science, you have a taste for elaborate tangles: the more intricate and difficult it is to dismantle, the happier you seem to be. You disregard the power of your heart and let your intellect lead you by the nose. There is another way. . . .

The essence of H-A's teaching to the Atlanteans is that the world is at a very critical stage in its evolution, yet a very exciting stage.

Every day is a special day at this moment in the evolution of this planet. As we limber up and move forward into the Aquarian Age, old standards are rapidly being replaced by new. It is a very difficult period. In some ways it is rather like the transitional period when a child starts to become an adult. It begins to experience emotions that hitherto it has not experienced, and which it does not fully understand. This is what is happening on your planet. On one side you have 'the establishment' at every level: political, spiritual, economic, every facet of collective life on Earth. On the other side you have a rebellion against the establishment, a reflection of today's reappraisal of long accepted standards and ideas.

The transitional period in the life of a teenager is very

delicate. It is a period in which the child has to be treated with great understanding and the parents prepared for sudden outbursts and rejections. The child kicks out against that which inside him he loves because he is trying to find himself. This is what is happening on your planet at the present time, for it is the culmination of so many things. You have this 'coming of age' of man. You have the re-emergence of Michael as the rightful guardian of this planet, and you have the transition from the Piscean to the Aquarian Age. These three tumultuous happenings have come together at the same time. This is the esoteric meaning of the astrological signs in the heavens, of that which has been written by seers and prophets many hundreds of years ago.

All forms of experience are becoming exaggerated and this is something you all must learn to understand and to cope with. All over the world people are becoming sensitive to the changes taking place and to the gathering momentum; they are becoming subconsciously aware of the unfolding evolution of the planet. In most cases they do not understand what it is that is motivating them. All they know is that they feel a restlessness and that what their father knew and accepted is no longer good enough. So you get frustration.

It is easy to argue that cities and urban sprawl are major causes of disruption and dissatisfaction but, if you really look at what is happening in depth, you will find that this restlessness goes much deeper. If you come out of the cities and go into the country, you will find there is the same restlessness, the same inability to be resigned and static. There are tremendous changes taking place on Earth and it is important that at this time we all try to understand them. One should never be frightened or fearful of change, neither should one desire change for its own sake. These next decades are critical in the evolution of the planet. You are witnessing the transformation of planet Earth: the whole planet is about to take a large step forward.

Twenty-five years ago H-A gave a warning of what we are doing to our world and what could happen if we do not pull our socks up and try to do something positive in the way we treat the planet and each other. Now we begin to see some of the consequences he predicted. The Earth, says H-A, is at a cross-roads. Which way will it go? The path of love, selflessness and responsibility, or the path of greed and destruction? According to H-A the pressures on the planet in this situation are immense. Spiritual evolution is not easy, because the wider you look in either direction the more difficult it is to maintain that very delicate balance in between. It is only from the centre of any situation that you can truly perceive all the aspects. As the planet goes forward into this Aquarian age, so it becomes pulled in either direction.

If this delicate balance can be found by your world, it will emerge into the next century into a most beautiful level of experience. If that balance fails, if the pendulum swings in the other direction, you could have catastrophe. I am not going to paint you dramatic pictures of the skies being rent and torn assunder. I am merely going to say to you, look at the ecological balance of this planet.

Man has to learn that he is not supreme on this planet. In fact, his behaviour is a shining example of immaturity. Apart from animals, fish life and birds, you have other forms of experience that express themselves through plants, trees and flowers: then you have the elemental spirits themselves. People on this planet are beginning to wake up to the danger of disregarding the elements of fire, earth, air and water. Man regards these things as his heritage and claims his right to use them. Man can use them, but he has not the right to abuse them.

Clearly man has to become very much less apathetic than he is now. More and more animals are being experimented on every year. More and more inhumane methods of slaughter are developed. What for? Quicker profits? How many of you really care or do anything about it? You can apply that throughout your life. If man can save money, he is perfectly happy to place toxic chemicals in his food. If he can make a food look and taste more attractive so that people will spend money on it, he has no hesitation in including a toxic substance to colour it or increase the amount of flavour by artificial additives. When a farmer farms his land, does he think in terms of the natural balance that lies within the soil? Or does he think in terms of the extra yield and larger grains of wheat he can produce? When you harness a new form of energy flow how far do you consider its relationship to the ecology of the planet? Do you just look at it as another resource for mankind? How fair is man to planet Earth? How fair is man to himself?

There are many ways and means of raising energy which can be justified inasmuch as they give respect to the other forms of experience. You have forms of energy all around you. You have the sun, you have the wind, you have the water, all of which could be utilised to give ample energy to the planet without abusing natural laws and creating poisonous waste. What other forms of energy do you need? But no one can make a profit out of selling the sun. *That* is your problem. It is not a scientific problem that you face on your planet, it is a problem of big business, of money and greed. Man is beginning to reap a very serious karma for himself, for the rest of mankind, for the future. The seasons are being affected and plants and trees are dying. The rainfall is out of balance: the rain is falling where it should not and it is not falling where it should.

Indeed, says H-A, unless mankind learns quickly to become responsible in its behaviour towards the ecological balance, very rapidly catstrophe can begin to approach. The balance of this planet is a very delicate one and the choice is with us, with each individual soul incarnate at this present time. We must start now to get things right for the rest of our time here and for the future of our children. Not only is man unconcerned about respect for other forms of experience, he also lacks generosity in his treatment of fellow human beings.

Your lives as a whole, the general running of the world today—even, in certain instances, your religion— are all based on competition, a striving for status, power and position, almost always at the expense of others. It is as if man has been unwilling to let go of the notion of 'survival of the fittest' and has carried it with him all the way from those primeval forests and jungles up to the present day, into his personal, emotional, family, professional, social, political and even spiritual lives. Why should this be so?

Fear. Fear of the unknown, fear of being beaten, outrun, outdone, threatened, attacked, even destroyed. At the personal level such thinking has always led to rivalry, suspicion, hatred, intrigue, violence and murder. At the tribal, racial and international levels it has led to vendetta, espionage, invasion, terrorism, war and genocide. How could it be otherwise? From your earliest years you are programmed to strive to be cleverer, faster, stronger, prettier, slimmer, richer, more attractive, more successful than the next person. You are conditioned to seek a better job, higher salary, bigger house or apartment, more possessions and more influential friends than the next person.

As a direct result of all this, a great many people suffer from some form of inferiority complex, and, in compensation, seek any means to bolster their egos. They resent richer, more successful and more powerful people and delight in watching them tumble off their pedestals. This fear and suspicion, this basic feeling of insecurity expresses itself through the personality of man as greed and an insane desire for power: power over one's fellow beings in an effort to balance out the insecurity. People become convinced that their beliefs, religion and way of life are the only possible ones. They dismiss others out of hand and are offended because you cannot accept what they have said. Perhaps they are hurt because secretly they feel you are somehow 'better' than they are and they feel inadequate. So they dig their heels in and cling to their beliefs and their intolerance for all the worst possible reasons.

Have you ever considered the major role that fear has played and still plays in the unfoldment of this planet? Corrupt men and regimes have always sought to control the people in their power. And what better way to achieve this than by using fear?

Fear of living, fear of poverty, fear of war, fear of reprisals and perhaps, above all, fear of death and nothingness. The result is that untold generations have lost heart, lost the will to question and explore, resigned themselves to monotony and debt and servitude: and, believing they have nothing to look forward to, have become like clay in the hands of ruthless men who have sent them to work and to war, for centuries on end. There has been a cruel and inexcusable manipulation of minds, souls, and lives. Great nations at this very moment rule by fear because their rulers are afraid. How sad one feels for them...the karma these rulers are piling up for themselves...the hell they will create within because they have not the courage to look forward...the mistake of thinking that security lies in armaments, in wealth and in worldly goods.

The breaking down of these traditional and conventional ways of thinking must take place. Countries must move away from the power concept, from denying their citizens the right to exercise free will. The only security in the universe is that which lies within, the spiritual security of knowing yourself. Each one of you is created thought with the free will to choose your experience absolutely. What greater security can any man seek? And those who do find security within have to learn to live in this world and to accept its material terms. You have to accept that some still need to rule by fear but, *because* you have found that inner security and have seen the light, you are able to forgive them and love them.

This is the true significance of the transition from the hidden qualities of the Piscean Age to the openness of the Aquarian Age. It is the supreme *moment of forgiveness*, when the forces of light are being brought to bear on your planet. Some people mistakenly think that by going along to a society like the Atlanteans they can find salvation from possible physical catastrophes. They are still creating the wrong priorities. The right priorities are finding the forces of love and forgiveness within, in order to step forward and set an example without fear.

Respect for other people's point of view is one of the prime ingredients for a contented and balanced life. The only way to save mankind from perishing on this planet is for man to overcome his inferiority complex and lack of security and learn the comfort and warmth of love, trust, understanding and, above all, respect for all other forms of experience around him. Unless he does so, it will not only be mankind who will suffer, but the plant life, the animals, the minerals. So much of Earth will suffer and is suffering through the selfishness and ignorance of man.

It is of paramount importance that man begins to look at the universe as a whole, that he begins to realise his place. The universe is just like a big family and if you have a family where everyone pulls together and helps one another, then everything runs smoothly, simply, and life is rich and full of happiness and understanding. If you have a family where one pulls this way and another only thinks of himself and pulls that way, then the harmony becomes disharmony. Unhappiness is set up, the balance of the physical bodies of the people themselves is affected and illness may very well result through the lack of harmony.

With the arrival of the Aquarian age, more and more ideas are being beamed down to mankind, says H-A, resulting in a general upsurge or awakening of consciousness. Recollections of races long forgotten, fragments of experience undergone in previous lives, are flooding in. Also rising to the surface are memories of Atlantis and the healing, science, art, knowledge and happiness that were known there. This is an inheritance which is not to be dismissed or ignored. We must begin to move away from the attitudes and thoughtforms of the last two thousand years, during which the physical and emotional natures of man were predominant, and on into the New Age, whose chief purpose will be the mastery of our own minds.

The paradox of mankind's development is that whenever there is great advancement in one area, a deterioration almost invariably occurs in another. The wise, bearing in mind the duality which characterises this system, will recognise and anticipate this phenomenon. As you pass through each successive life here on Earth, you will gradually master the art of selection and discrimination.

This process will strengthen your ability to remain steadfast to your choice. Temptations and distractions will always be there, but as your sense of 'what is right for me' continues to develop, you will no longer care if those around you, indulging themselves in various ways, shout 'Coward, you don't know what you're missing!' For that is just the point; by this time you *will* know what you are missing, and you will be only too glad to miss it. By this time you will be in contact with your higher self, which will already be offering you vistas and perspectives, adventures and experiences, compared with which the trends and indulgences of the day are very small fry indeed.

With the evolution of the brain and the physical body and the expansion of the ego within man, much has been learned during recent centuries and, in particular, during this century. Man has gained knowledge of nuclear power, the atom and the fundamental physical structure of all things. He has learned much about electronics. He is beginning to rediscover certain ways of using sound and vibration and how all these things play a part in the universe. He has begun to understand time in relation to other dimensions. The accumulation of knowledge, H-A points out, needs to be tempered with wisdom and responsibility:

> The Earth is like a snowball which is all the time gathering in size, increasing in experience and knowledge and, we hope, understanding. For knowledge is responsibility; it becomes an asset only if it is used with wisdom and understanding. The more one experiences, the more one understands and so one evolves. This applies not only to man, but to all the other kingdoms, the solar systems and the galaxy. All advancement carries the penalty of responsibility. In seeing more, hearing more, knowing more, the challenge is whether you can translate this seeing, hearing and knowing into *understanding*, and fully accept the responsibility inherent in that understanding.

As your knowledge expands you may see vistas that you do not *want* to understand, vistas that depress you. Yet somehow, through this maelstrom of emotion and confused thinking you have to seek and clarify and, in so doing, grow and evolve. You have to recognise also that you can only grow and evolve by virtue of all the other forms of experience around you: that you have to go through initiations in life and that evolution is not a long straight line, a gentle incline up which to saunter forth at a steady pace. Experience is not like that, for free will, your spiritual heritage, also means that you have to experience the free will of all other beings that surround you at any one moment in time. That is quite a thought! As you taste that experience you go through forms of initiation, pillars of understanding, gateways that open out new vistas for you. And as you do this as individuals, so the planet as a whole undergoes initiations.

The key to world harmony lies not in having one universal religion, says H-A. It is in man coming to terms with himself, in realising and accepting his own incompleteness:

> The rhythm in which humanity is moving at this present time is a period in which people are beginning to approach each other in their understanding of the universe. It would be quite wrong to try to force a dominant view of spirituality on mankind today.
> There have been many prophecies made about another coming of the Christ. What is happening, however, is a little different from the one single figure who might emerge as a world visionary or leader, because present day experience is moving beyond that concept. You are moving into a concept of wholeness. This 'second coming' of the Christos, the Christ spirit, is taking place right now. It is here amongst you at this

very moment, bringing wisdom and light wherever people are ready to receive it and it is coinciding with the emergence of the Aquarian age. The emergence comes through inspiration in many different ways. Hundreds of new societies and groups and religions are springing up. Witness the enormous interest breaking out as we enter the 'New Age'; the last thirty years has been the tip of the iceberg.

There is a tremendous amount of love being generated. Love is the only true and lasting way to overcome negativity and fear. There is no other solution. This is a beautiful planet, a planet of colour, of music, a planet so rich in vegetation that there is something for everyone. Why should man allow greed and envy and fear to spoil that picture? It is a question of educating people into what love really is. Love is not the stimulation of the physical senses: it is the attunement of your whole being, your physical body, subtle bodies and your higher self into one glowing being where, within you, you have the security of God's love. Let us use it and give it forth. If you believe in your divinity, if you believe that there is a God of love, in some small way you can play a part in these things by seeing people for what they are and feeling for them, yet not condemning them. Understanding and accepting others is not an expression of weakness, it is the greatest expression of strength.

This is a time when spiritual seeking and understanding is growing right down at the grass roots level, where it is up to each individual to find himself and his own spiritual path and, in finding himself, to help others along *their* way. You are never going to do it through criticism, through feeling superior or inferior, by comparing, by feeling jealousy, hatred, contempt, anger or by seeking power. All those roads are so easy. Pride and prejudice must be swept out of the window, not with the yard-broom but with love; not with force or determination, but by creating the right circumstances with love and understanding so that they no longer need to exist.

There are no short cuts. It requires individual and collective effort in harmony, working together, sharing together. You have to retain individual and national personalities, and yet break down individual and national barriers. You have to learn not to judge your neighbour. You need a kind of inner determination to find that light within you, and with it the will to spread it in the right way. It is not easy, giving forth light, it is not easy finding the light for the spiritual path is very rocky, full of hidden traps that will find your Achilles heel very quickly. But the rewards are great. The rewards can be fantastic if you give yourself to the momentum and remain calm.

Remember, says H-A, you do not have to do or be anything in this universe, the choice is always yours. You have been given the free will to steer your evolution as you wish.

Strange as it may seem, the future of this planet is not pre-determined; in fact you are creating that future all the time by your every thought, action and deed, and this is why the spreading of light is so important. One does not have to convert or force anyone. Every single person can play their part for, if you meditate and send out light every day, then you are making a significant contribution to the future: you are affecting the future. *You are the future.* All those incarnate at this time are truly privileged for this is one of the most interesting periods in the history and evolution of planet Earth and you are part of that history, part of that evolution.

Earth as a whole has to find its rhythm once again, and we can help it by harmonising within ourselves with love and then extending that love and harmony to the planet as a whole. This is the way to find world peace. This is the way to help Michael resume his rightful position as guardian Deva of planet Earth. This is the way to know true joy, true peace and a feeling of expansion within us which reaches right into the universe.

It is at times like this that the spiritual realms bring tremendous pressures to bear, and rightly so, says H-A. The Godhead can only offer love and spiritual understanding, it cannot offer personal power, personal achievement. As we enter the Aquarian Age, H-A and other spirits of light have tried to bring down a love vibration that will help people. Not force them, but help them as they open their hearts and minds and souls to receive that love, so that it vibrates within them.

The angelic forces obviously wish to see mankind rise above the need for catastrophe, to rise above the need for war, torture and suffering. None of these things are God-wished. The sooner mankind can come to that realisation, the safer the planet will become, ecologically and in every way. You have the free will, it is your decision. You are in a climactic situation, a situation that in my opinion could go either way. The challenge is yours. In the past fifteen to twenty years we have been very happy to see the way mankind has begun to respond to our message, and in many ways the possibility of catastrophe is less now that it was a few years ago. But it is not the time for complacency; it is the time for renewed commitment and effort. You cannot run away from problems and those with a true spiritual motivation will be those who stay put, knowing that the security lies not on top of a mountain, nor in a cave but inside you, in communion with your own higher self. In the coming years it will require even greater efforts on the part of those working for the forces of light to spread spiritual understanding.

When the human race as a whole emerges into the full light of the coming age, when it reacquaints itself with such basic aspects of universal law as karma, reincarnation and self-responsibility *and* begins to instil this wisdom into its children, such follies as ruthless competition, hoarding of resources, pride, intrigue, espionage and war will fade into your memories: memories of a long and troubled and mercifully receding past. A far more rewarding set of principles and activities will replace them, including: self-acceptance and self-respect, thinking for oneself; respect for others and their opinions and beliefs, regardless of race or religion; respect for the planet and all forms of life; education based on the development of the human personality and the encouragement of individual talents and aptitudes, both inner and outer; business based on mutual advantage; investigation of what people have in common, rather than what appears to separate them, and a pooling of their talents and resources for the common good; a growing acquaintance with the ancient wisdom; insights into the material and subtle universe. And not a century too soon!

Time is short, for you are caught in this process of acceleration. Yet through your love, through your kindness and dedication, you have to remove the need for that acceleration. Not take it away, not stop it, not destroy it, but remove the need for it and gently guide this transformation from the adolescent Earth to the adult Earth. In guiding Earth through this stage of spiritual puberty, you will learn to find yourselves as individuals, as whole beings.

This transformation *is* possible. I urge all of you who read this to assess yourselves, to see yourselves for what you are, to learn to love yourselves for what you are and to go forth to spread light and love to your neighbours, to your friends, to animals, to all the kingdoms existing on this planet, before it is too late. In bringing this light you will help others to regain respect for all that abounds on this great planet, for all that is part of you.

Shall we begin?

The Sanctuary, Runnings Park

Afterword

By Helio-Arcanophus

This is a story about an impulse; an impulse of energy that has drawn people together; an impulse of energy that has united a group of people in race memory, helping them to find an avenue of fulfilment in their lives. I have had the honour of being the focus of that impulse.

It has been said that there is nothing new in the universe. Like most statements this is both correct and incorrect. It is correct in the sense that spirits within a human body have the opportunity to live out in physical life some of the spiritual energies within them. It is incorrect, in the sense that those energies have been created by the Godhead and every energy that is created by that Godhead is unique. Each has its own quality; it has its own understanding, its own perception. Through its beingness it experiences, and as those experiences accumulate, so that spiritual energy evolves, gathers wisdom, bringing about a movement towards the infinite harmony that is the Godhead itself. It takes many lives to find that infinite harmony and during this process spirits tend to group together to work out a kind of group karma, learning and experiencing together, sharing each other's happiness, sharing each other's unhappiness.

This is what evolution is all about, and I hope that as you have read this book you, too, have been able to share in some of the adventures that these people have been through. As I have watched them grow I have loved them; I have forgiven them; I have encouraged them to forgive themselves. For in that forgiveness they have found their love for their fellow beings. And in that love they have found a simple philosophy of life; a simple philosophy of the universe that has helped them and is helping them to make their contribution towards the emergence of the Aquarian Age, a vital moment in the evolution of your planet, a high watermark in all the emotional traumas that your world has gone through and for all the beings that live on it.

For without forgiveness there is no hope for future peace and love. Wars are fought through pride, fear, intolerance, being frightened to stand down and say "Maybe I'm wrong". This need not be denigration or weakness. This is the fundamental strength behind which the whole basis of spiritual doctrine is made. God does not judge. It is man who judges. Man must create himself in God's image, not expect God to create himself in man's image.

This is the kind of message that I hope this book will bring to you; a message of total acceptance; a message of total tolerance; a simple message for mankind about working together, not in anger but in love. Of all the planets in God's universe, Earth in my opinion is one of the most interesting because it represents extremes of good and evil, of black and white that are more diametrically opposed than any other level of experience in the universe. You can see it in your music, for example; how some music flows and inspires you, how some music tears you apart. You can see it in your art. You can see it in your literature. You can see it in your fellow beings.

But I did not wish this book to be only about a spiritual teaching. I wished that it could be about the adventures, the growing up, the awareness of a small group of people who came together, joining their energies, which enabled me to bring forth some ideas that are contemporary with the mood of present day civilisation. No teaching can claim to be right or unique. It can only offer an aspect of truth as it is seen in the eyes of those who perpetrate it and give it forth. I can offer no more. All teachings of light contain aspects of truth. For truth is universal; truth is absolute. But who is in a position to understand truth until they have found that level of love and wisdom that is the Godhead itself?

I hope that you can find sympathy with some of their frustrations, the difficulties that they have gone through. I would like you to look at those difficulties and frustrations not as problems but as initiations, steps they have taken that have helped them to grow in their awareness. Steps that have enabled them to see the truth behind my teaching and the truth behind all teachings of the Godhead.

So this is a book about love, love on all dimensions. I would like to feel that this book will highlight some of your own difficulties, some of your own initiations and help you to find your awareness, whether it be through the type of approach that I have offered or through some other philosophy, sect or religion that is meaningful to you. I hope that you have enjoyed the humour, for there is much happiness and humour within the universe and it is important that we all share in this and feel the exhilaration, the excitement, the wonder of it all.

Have you ever thought about some of these things before? Do you think that you might have lived in a physical body before; have you experienced that feeling of déjà vu? Do you find God an enigma? Do you find *life* an enigma? Have you suffered very much in your life? Have you asked yourself why? Suffering is so often brought on by our own thoughts, actions and deeds. In one sense it is a state of mind because whatever problem you are trying to live through, it is one that can be overcome by the heightening of your own inspiration, by lifting yourself above the morass of physical existence, by accepting physical existence, by seeing it for what it is, no more no less. This, dear friends, is the starting point for true spiritual revelation. You don't have to become a monk or a saint. You are all monks; you are all saints if you want to be.

Finally, may I say that I hope that you have enjoyed reading this book as much as I have enjoyed seeing it being created. If you have any questions about it, then I am sure that some of those concerned and written about in the book will be delighted to answer them for you.

Thank you and bless you.

The Atlanteans
Runnings Park
Croft Bank
West Malvern
Worcs. WR14 4BP

If you'd like to learn more about H-A's teaching, why not try:

THE GUIDE BOOK: The Teaching of Helio-Arcanophus
Channelled by Tony Neate
Edited and arranged by Michael Dean

"How much simpler life would be if we all arrived here wearing a small book of instructions round our neck – which we could consult whenever a problem or challenge crops up...", says Robert Donaldson. A comment that inspired Michael Dean to compile this material which answers such fundamental questions as:

  'Where have I come from?'
  'Why am I here?'
  'What is the purpose of human existence?'
  'Are unseen intelligences working alongside the human race?'
  'Is there a universal law?'
  'Where so we go from here?'

Michael came across the material in the late '60s and found that it not only provided answers to many of the enigmas that face mankind today, but presented in a very simple and direct way a comprehensive and encouraging picture of our place in the scheme of things. To these earlier teachings of Helio-Arcanophus he has added more recent lectures, to make a handbook for every man, woman and young person.

  H. A. has made prophesies which time and events have proved right. But this message is not a prophecy of doom; it is a challenge for mankind to come to terms with his fellow beings and to treat the planet with respect. The teachings are enjoying a fast growing readership in Britain, in Europe, in North America and elsewhere.

224 pp   hardcover   £7.95

Obtainable through your bookseller, or if you have difficulty, through Gateway Books *or through* The Atlanteans.

A wide range of books dealing with the many challenges and opportunities of this crucial planetary moment are obtainable from:

Pegasus Book Service
Runnings Park
Croft Bank
West Malvern
Worcestershire WR14 4BP
England

Tel: 06845 65253

and also from:

The Whole Bookshop
197 Piccadilly
London W1

Tel: 01-734 7449